I said it My Way

THE GUINNESS DICTIONARY OF
HUMOROUS
MISQUOTATIONS

— COMPILED BY COLIN JARMAN —

I said it My Way

THE GUINNESS DICTIONARY OF
HUMOROUS
MISQUOTATIONS

— COMPILED BY COLIN JARMAN —

GUINNESS PUBLISHING

Design and Layout: Stonecastle Graphics Ltd

Copyright © Colin M. Jarman

First published in 1994 by Guinness Publishing Ltd,
Publication copyright © Guinness Publishing Ltd 1994
Published in Great Britain by Guinness Publishing Ltd,
33 London Road, Enfield, Middlesex

Typeset in Times and Helvetica by Ace Filmsetting Ltd, Frome, Somerset
Printed and bound in Great Britain by Cox & Wyman Ltd, Reading

'Guinness' is a registered trade mark of Guinness Publishing Ltd

A catalogue record for this book is available from the British Library.

ISBN 0–85112–784–3

" INTRODUCTION "

A widely-read man never quotes accurately . . . Misquotation is the pride and privilege of the learned . . . . Misquotations are the only quotations that are never misquoted.

Hesketh Pearson *Common Misquotations*

Famous remarks are seldom quoted correctly.

Simeon Strunsky *No Mean City* (1944)

It is gentlemanly to get one's quotations very slightly wrong. In that way one unprigs oneself and allows the company to correct one.

Lord Ribblesdale *The Light of Common Day*

Take hackneyed jokes from Miller, got by rote,
With just enough of learning to misquote.

Lord Byron *English Bards and Scotch Reviewers*

Quotation: the act of repeating erroneously the words of another.

Ambrose Bierce *The Devil's Dictionary* (1911)

It is better to be quotable than to be honest.

Tom Stoppard *The Guardian* (1973)

What is a *humorous misquotation*? A well-known saying or phrase . . .

To be or not to be, that is the question. William Shakespeare

- that has been rearranged, redefined or revamped (however slightly) with a humorous, witty or pithy consequence . . .

T. B. or not T. B., that is congestion. Woody Allen

There are a number of different types of misquotation that bring a fresh meaning to an old saying. A few basic examples are:

a. The single letter change –

Mon<u>k</u>ey is the root of all evil. Anon

b. The single word change –

Actions <u>lie</u> louder than words. Carolyn Wells

c. The changed ending –

There'll always be an England – <u>even if it's in Hollywood.</u> Bob Hope

d. The multiple change –

A thing of <u>duty</u> is a <u>boy</u> forever. Flann O'Brien

There are many other forms of misquotation to be found in this book, including well-known puns, spoonerisms and malapropisms.

Some authors, who appear more regularly than others, seem to have made an art of humorous misquotation – most notably Oscar Wilde, who used misquotes as a French chef uses garlic. Old faithfuls such as Dorothy Parker, Groucho Marx and Ogden Nash are joined by modern masters of the misquote, such as Woody Allen, Bill Cosby, Fran Lebowitz, Robin Williams, Spike Milligan and Quentin Crisp. Denis Nordern and Frank Muir went a stage further in developing their own brand of misquote to provide punchlines for their short stories on BBC Radio's *My Word*. Some of the less likely misquoters included in this book are Joan Collins, George Best, Jimmy Saville and Sarah Ferguson.

At the end of some of the batches of quotes I have made my own suggestions for misquotations which occurred to me during the compilation of this volume.

With apologies to Tom Stoppard:

It is better to be misquotable than to be honest.

Colin M. Jarman

❝ EDITORIAL NOTES ❞

I Said It My Way has three sections:

1. A main section of misquotations arranged alphabetically by key word. Each batch of misquotes contains a 'base quote' (the source of the misquotes) in bold type – followed by the various misquotes (in chronological order, where applicable). The base quote is not necessarily the earliest form of the saying in question, but rather its most commonly occurring usage.

2. Thematic boxes spread throughout the main section. Many of these misquotes are not derived from one single source, but are variants on the same theme. For example, 'Jolly Mixtures' (pp. 107 and 117) are sections of mixed metaphors, malapropisms and verbal gaffes.

3. Index of authors.

" CONTENTS **"**

KEY WORD
ABHORS • AFRAID • AGAINST • AGE • ALWAYS • ANGELS • ANGER
ANGRY • ANOTHER • ARMY • ARROW • ART • ASHES
BAD • BALLS • BATTLE • BEAT • BEAUTIFUL • BEAUTY • BED
BEDFELLOWS • BEE • BEGGARS • BEHIND • BELIEVING • BEST
BETTER • BIRD • BITE • BLESSED • BLIND • BODY • BORN • BOW
BOY • BRAVE • BREAD • BRIDGE • BULL • BUSINESS • BUTTER
CAKE • CALL • CAME • CAN • CANDY • CAN'T • CARE • CASTLE
CAT • CAUSE • CHARITY • CHILD • CHILDREN • CHIP • CHIPS
CHOSEN • CHRISTMAS • CIRCUMVENT • CITY • CLASSES
CLEANLINESS • CLOSED • CLOTHES • CLOTHING • CLOUD • COALS
COMEDY • COMMITTEE • COMPANY • CORRUPTS • COUNTED
COUNTRY • COW • CRIME • CRY • CULTURE • CURSE
DARKEN • DAY • DEAD • DEATH • DELIGHTFUL • DEVIL • DIE
DISCOVERED • DISTANCE • DO • DOG • DOING • DONKEY • DOUBT
DO UNTO . . . • DREAMS • DRESSED • DRINK • DRUM • DRY
DUCK • DUTY
EAGLE • EAR • EAST • EAT • EGGS • ELECTRA • ENCOUNTERS
END • ENGLAND • EQUAL • EVIL • EXIST • EXPANDS • EYES
FACE • FAIR • FAITH • FAMILIARITY • FAMILIES • FAMILY • FAT
FATHER • FAVOUR • FEAR • FEED • FEET • FEMALE • FIRE • FLAG
FOLD • FOOL • FOOT • FORGIVE • FREE • FREEZE • FRENCH
FRIEND • FRIGHTEN • FUGITIVE • FUN • FUNNY • FUTURE
GAME • GAS • GENIUS • GENTLEMEN • GIFT • GIVE • GLASSES
GLITTERS • GO • GOD • GOOD • GOVERNMENT • GRAPES
GREATEST • GRIN • GROW
HABITS • HALF • HAMLET • HAND • HANG • HAPPINESS • HASTE
HAVE • HEAD • HEALTH • HEART • HEAT • HEAVEN • HELL • HELP
HERE • HERO • HESITATES • HIDE • HISTORY • HOME • HONESTY
HOPE • HOUSE • HOW • HUMAN • HURT • HUSH
IF • IGNORANCE • IMITATE • INHUMANITY • INNOCENT
INSULT • . . . ISM
JUDGE • JUSTICE
KEEP • KNOW

LACE • LAMPPOST • LAND • LAUGH • LAURELS • LEAD • LEGEND
LET • LIBERAL • LIE • LIES • LIFE • LIGHTNING • LION • LITTLE
LOOK • LORD • LOSE • LOT • LOUDER • LOVE
MAD • MAGNIFIQUE • MAN • MARRIAGE • MEEK • MESS • MICE
MILK • MIND • MIRROR • MISTAKES • MONEY • MONKEYS
MONTH • MOTHER • MOULD • MOUNTAIN • MOUTH • MURDER
MUSIC • MYSTERIOUS
NAKED • NATION • NEVER • NEWS • NICE • NIGHT • NONSENSE
NOTHING
OBEYED • OBSCENITY • OFFER • OIL • ONCE • ONE • OPPORTUNITY
OUT • OVER • OYSTER
PAINT • PAY • PEN • PENNY • PEOPLE • PLAGUE • POACHERS
POLITICS • PORTRAIT • POT • POUR • POVERTY • POWER
PRESIDENT • PRESS • PROOF • PUBLIC • PUBLISH • PUNCTUALITY
PURE • PURSE • PURSUIT • PUT
QUESTION
RACE • RAIDER • REAL • REBEL • RECESSION • REFUGE
REPRESENTATION • RICH • RIGHT • ROOST • ROOT • ROPE • ROSE
SAFE • SAID • SALT • SAY • SCRATCH • SCUM • SECRET • SEE
SERVE • SHALT • SHEPHERD • SHOE • SHORT • SHOW ME . . .
SIDES • SIGH • SILENCE • SINCEREST • SINS • SKELETON • SLAVES
SLICE • SMOKE • SOFT • SOFTLY • SOLD • SOLDIERS • SORROW
SORRY • SOUL • SOUND • SPACE • SPADE • SPEAK • SPOIL • SPREAD
STAGE • STAND • STATESMAN • STONE • STOPS • STORM • STRAW
STRIKE • SUCCEED • SUMMER • SUN • SUPPORT • SURVIVAL
SWEET • SWING
TAILORS • TAKE • TALK • TEACH • TEACHER • THIEF • THINK
THINKING • TIGER • TIME • TODAY AND TOMORROW • TOOLS
TOP • TOUGH • TRAGEDY • TREE • TRIUMPH • TROUBLE
TRUMPET • TRUST • TRUTH • TWO
UGLY • UNDERSTANDING
VARIETY • VICTOR • VIRTUE • VOICE
WAGES • WAITS • WALKS • WALL • WAR • WASH • WATER • WEB
WHEAT • WHITE • WHO • WHOLE • WIFE • WILL • WIND • WINE
WINNING • WINTER • WOMAN • WON OR LOST • WOODPILE
WORD • WORK • WORLD • WRONG

" ABHORS "

NATURE ABHORS A VACUUM.

FRANCOIS RABELAIS *GARGANTUA* (1534)

Nature abhors a virgin – a frozen asset. Clare Booth Luce

Nature adores a virgin. Anon

The world's most abhorred vacuum is in the pocketbook. Anon

" AFRAID "

WHO'S AFRAID OF THE BIG BAD WOLF?

CHILDREN'S SONG TITLE

Who's Afraid of Virginia Woolf? Edward Albee *Play title* (1962)

Me, I'm afraid of Virginia Woolf. Alan Bennett *Play title* (1978)

" AGAINST "

WE'RE NOT ONE BIT MORE SINNED AGAINST THAN SINNING.

ARISTOPHANES (410 BC)

I am a man more dined against than dining. Sir Maurice Bowra

He makes you feel more danced against than with. Sally Poplin

" AGE "

AGE BEFORE BEAUTY.

ANON SAYING

Age before beauty . . . swine before pearls. Dorothy Parker

Age before beauty . . . dust before broom. Anon

Age before beauty . . . men before monkeys. Anon

Age before duty. Anon

AGE CANNOT WITHER HER, NOR CUSTOM STALE HER INFINITE VARIETY.

WILLIAM SHAKESPEARE *ANTONY AND CLEOPATRA* (1607)

On Peggy Eaton – Age cannot wither her, nor custom stale her infinite virginity. Daniel Webster

On Marlene Dietrich – Age cannot wither her, nor custom stale her infinite sameness. David Shipman

Age cannot wither me. Sergio Leone *Once Upon a Time in America* (1984)

ADVERTS I

BREAKFAST IN LONDON. LUNCH IN NEW YORK.

BRITISH AIRWAYS

. . . and luggage in Bermuda.   Graffiti

THE FRENCH ADORE LE PIAT D'OR.   PIAT D'OR WINE

Les Francais abhorrent le Piat D'or.   Andrew Barr *Time Out* (1992)

HEINEKEN REFRESHES THE PARTS OTHER BEERS CANNOT REACH.   TERRY LOVELOCK for HEINEKEN LAGER

Heineken refreshes the partridges other beers cannot reach.

Lord Carrington is the peer who reaches those foreign parts other
peers cannot reach.   Margaret Thatcher

Courage reaches the parts other beers don't bother with.   Graffiti

Joe Jordan kicks the parts other beers cannot reach.   Graffiti

Vindaloo purges the parts other curries cannot reach.   Graffiti

JOIN THE ARMY. SEE THE WORLD. MEET INTEREST-ING PEOPLE.   ARMY ENROLMENT SLOGAN

Join the Army and see the Navy.   Marx Brothers *Duck Soup* (1933)

Join the Army. See the world. Meet interesting people – and kill them.
1960s pacifist slogan

MAKE SOMEONE HAPPY – RING THEM.   B.T. ADVERT

Make someone happy – wring Buzby's neck!   Graffiti

POLO: THE MINT WITH A HOLE.   ADVERT

After the Royal Mint had relocated to Llantrisant in Wales –
Llantrisant is the hole with a Mint.   Graffiti

SAY IT WITH FLOWERS.   P. F. O'KEEFE (1917)

Say it with flowers . . . Buy her an olive branch.   Anon

Say it with flowers . . . Buy her a triffid.   Graffiti

STOP ME AND BUY ONE.   WALLS' ICE CREAM SLOGAN (1934)

Buy me and stop one.   Graffiti on a condom machine

WHISKAS – NINE OUT OF TEN OWNERS SAID THEIR CATS PREFERRED IT.   WHISKAS CAT FOOD

Nine out of ten whiskers said their owners preferred it.
Panasonic Wet-Dry shaver advert (1993)

Bestiality – Nine out ten cats said their owners preferred it.   Graffiti

—— ❝ ALWAYS ❞ ——

IT IS ALWAYS DARKEST BEFORE THE DAWN.

THOMAS FULLER *PISGAH SIGHT* (1650)

It is always dullest before the yawn.

Bob Philips

—— ❝ ANGELS ❞ ——

**HARK! THE HERALD ANGELS SING,
GLORY TO THE NEW-BORN KING,
PEACE ON EARTH AND MERCY MILD,
GOD AND SINNERS RECONCILED!** CHARLES WESLEY (1742)

Hark! the herald angels sing
Beecham's pills are just the thing.
Peace on earth and mercy mild;
Two for man and one for child.

Anon

—— ❝ ANGER ❞ ——

LOOK BACK IN ANGER. JOHN OSBORNE *PLAY TITLE* (1956)

Headline concerning an Essex library strike – Book Lack In Ongar.

Private Eye

—— ❝ ANGRY ❞ ——

**WHEN ANGRY, COUNT TEN BEFORE YOU SPEAK; IF
VERY ANGRY, COUNT ONE HUNDRED.**

THOMAS JEFFERSON *LETTER* (1817)

When angry, count to four; when very angry, swear. Mark Twain

When you get angry, they tell you to count to five before you reply.
  Why should I count to five? It's what happens before you count to
  five which makes life interesting. David Hare *Secret Rapture* (1988)

ADVERTS II

HAPPINESS IS A WARM EARPIECE.   BRITISH TELECOM

Yes . . . but ecstasy is a warm codpiece.   Graffiti

I'M MARGIE, FLY ME.   U.S. NATIONAL AIRLINES (1971)

I'm meaty, fry me.   Walls' Sausage advert

A MILLION HOUSEWIVES EVERY DAY, PICK UP A TIN OF BEANS AND SAY BEANZ MEANZ HEINZ!

    RUTH WATSON for HEINZ BAKED BEANS

Beanz Meanz Fartz!   Graffiti

NOTHING WORKS FASTER THAN ANADIN   ADVERT

If Nothing works faster than Anadin – use nothing.   Graffiti

TYPHOO PUT THE T INTO BRITAIN   TYPHOO TEA

Jazz put the sin into syncopation.   Anne Shaw Faulkner *Ladies' Home Journal*

Swindon put the Wilt in Wiltshire.   Mr. Hobbs

Gable puts the arson in Garson.   Hollywood publicity slogan

Garson puts the able into Gable.   Greer Garson

Who put the bomp in the bomp-a-bomp-a-bomp?

    Showaddywaddy *Song title* (1982)

Richard Nixon put the dick into radical.   Anon

Money puts the prop in propaganda.   Anon

If Typhoo put the T into Britain who put the Arse in Arsenal?   Graffiti

WE'LL TAKE MORE CARE OF YOU.   BRITISH AIRWAYS

British Airways: We'll take more fares off you.   Graffiti

YOU KNOW WHEN YOU'VE BEEN TANGO'D?

    TANGO ADVERT

You know when you've been quango'd?   *Spitting Image*

YOU'RE NEVER ALONE WITH A STRAND.

    CIGARETTE ADVERT

You're never alone with schizophrenia.   Graffiti

❝ ANOTHER ❞

ONE MAN'S MEAT IS ANOTHER MAN'S POISON.

TITUS LUCRETIUS *DE RERUM NATURA* (100 BC)

One man's poetry is another man's poison. Oscar Wilde

One man's news is another man's troubles. Finley Peter Dunne (1901)

One man's fish is another man's poisson. Carolyn Wells

One man's poison ivy is another man's spinach. George Ade (1920)

One man's Mede is another man's Persian. George S. Kaufman

One man's mate is another man's passion. Eugene Healy (1940)

One man's red tape is another man's system. Dwight Waldo (1946)

One man's cliché can be another man's conviction. Adlai Stevenson (1959)

One man's mate is another man's poison. Richard Gordon

One woman's poise is another woman's poison. Katherine Brush

One man's wage rise is another man's price increase. Harold Wilson

One man's meat is another woman's Sunday gone.

Mel Calman *Calman and Women* (1967)

One man's meat is a Doberman's paws on. Denis Nordern *My Word* (1980)

One man's ceiling is another man's floor. *Sunday Times*

❝ ARMY ❞

AN ARMY, LIKE A SERPENT, TRAVELS ON ITS BELLY.

FREDERICK THE GREAT Attrib.

An army marches on its stomach. Napoleon Bonaparate Attrib.

Napoleon's armies always used to march on their stomachs, shouting:
Vive l'interieur!' W. C. Sellar and R. J. Yeatman *1066 and All That*

❝ ARROW ❞

I SHOT AN ARROW IN THE AIR.
IT FELL TO EARTH, I KNOW NOT WHERE.

HENRY WADSWORTH LONGFELLOW *THE ARROW AND THE SONG*

I shot an arrow in the air – and it stuck. Anti-pollution slogan

AGES OF MANKIND

The seven ages of man –

6 weeks – all systems go
6 years – all systems *No!*
16 years – all systems know
26 years – all systems glow
36 years – all systems owe
56 years – all systems status quo
76 years – all systems slow.   R. M. Cornelius *The Rotarian*

A woman at the age of 12 is a sketch,
at 15 a drawing,
at 18 she paints herself and
at 20 she exhibits herself.
But whatever her age, she is never a still life.   Edgar Degas

At 16 I was stupid, confused, insecure and indecisive,
at 25 I was wise, self-confident, prepossessing and assertive,
at 45 I am stupid, confused, insecure and indecisive.
Who would have supposed that maturity is only a short break from
        adolescence.   Jules Feiffer (1974)

At 20 years of age the will reigns;
at 30 the wit;
at 40 the judgement.   Benjamin Franklin *Poor Richard's Almanac* (1741)

At twenty man is a peacock,
at thirty a lion,
at forty a camel,
at fifty a serpent,
at sixty a dog,
at seventy an ape,
at eighty nothing at all.   Baltasaar Gracian *The Art of Worldly Wisdom* (1647)

The vital stages of man: He believes in Father Christmas; he doesn't
        believe in Father Christmas; he is Father Christmas.   Jim Guthrie

At 18, one adores at once;
at 20, one loves;
at 30, one desires;
at 40, one reflects.   Paul de Kock

The four stages of man are infanthood, childhood, adolescence and
        obsolescence.   Art Linkletter *A Child's Garden of Misinformation* (1965)

The three ages of man: youth, middle age and 'you're looking wonderful!'   Francis J. Spellman

From birth to 18, a girl needs good parents.
From 18 to 35, she needs good looks.
From 35 to 55, good personality.
From 55 on, she needs good cash.
I'm saving my money.   Sophie Tucker

Childhood ends at 12
Youth at 18
Love at 20
Faith at 30
Hope at 40
Desire at 50.   German proverb

The four ages of man: 20-30 tri-weekly; 30-40 try weekly; 40-50 try
weakly; 50-60 Beer is best.   Anon

" ART "

ART FOR ART'S SAKE (*ARS GRATIA ARTIS*) LATIN PROVERB
Art for art's sake makes no more sense than gin for gin's sake.
                                                            W. Somerset Maugham

LIFE DOESN'T IMITATE ART.   SENECA (63)
Art doesn't imitate life, if only for fear of clichés.   Joseph Brodsky
Life doesn't imitate art. It imitates bad television.   Woody Allen

" ASHES "

WE COMMIT HIS BODY TO THE GROUND; EARTH TO EARTH, ASHES TO ASHES, DUST TO DUST.
                                              THE BOOK OF COMMON PRAYER (1662)

On Oscar Wilde – When Oscar came to join his God,
    Not earth to earth, but sod to sod.
  It was for sinners such as this
    Hell was created bottomless.   Algernon Charles Swinburne

Ashes to ashes, and clay to clay,
If the enemy don't get you, your own folks may.   James Thurber

On Dennis Lillee and Jeff Thomson (Australian fast bowlers) – Ashes to ashes, dust to dust,
If Lillee don't get you, Thomson must.   *Sydney Telegraph* (1975)

Ashes to ashes, dust to dust,
Never seen a woman a man could trust.   American Negro Song

Ashes to ashes, dust to dust,
If heaven doesn't get you, the other place must.   American Saying

Ashes to ashes, dust to dust;
If it wasn't for you, my cock would rust.   Anon

Ashes to ashes, dust to dust,
What is a sweater without a bust?   Anon

❝ BAD ❞

FROM GOOD TO BAD, AND FROM BAD TO WORSE.
EDMUND SPENSER *THE SHEPHEARDE'S CALENDER: FEBRUARY* (1579)

Some prose writers go from bad to verse.   *Columbia Record*

Some poets go from bard to verse.   Anon

'HOOK AND LADDER' – THE SORT OF SHOW THAT GIVES FAILURE A BAD NAME.   WALTER KERR

There are writers like Cyril Connolly who give pleasure a bad name.
E. M. Forster

'Oh Calcutta!' – The sort of show that gives pornography a bad name.
Clive Barnes

'Beast of the Yellow Night' (1970) – A film bad enough to give the Devil a bad name.   Alan Frank *Science Fiction Handbook* (1982)

'Sister Act' (1992) – The script is completely and utterly unfunny. It's enough to give feminism a bad name.   Ruth Picardie *Modern Review*

'Repo Man' (1984) – The sort of disjointed film that gives cult a bad name.   Simon Rose *Essential Film Guide* (1993)

❝ BALLS ❞

GOODNESS GRACIOUS, GREAT BALLS OF FIRE.
JERRY LEE LEWIS *SONG TITLE* (1957)

Goodness gracious, great balls of fur.   Rob Thompson *The Red Cat* (1993)

Windsor Castle – Great Halls of Fire.   Anon newspaper headline (1992)

❝ BATTLE ❞

THE BATTLE OF WATERLOO WAS WON ON THE PLAYING FIELDS OF ETON.
SIR WILLIAM FRASER (1889)

(*More commonly attributed to the Duke of Wellington*)

The Battle of Yorktown was lost on the playing fields of Eton.
H. Allen Smith

Probably the Battle of Waterloo *was* won on the playing fields of Eton, but the opening battles of all subsequent wars have been lost there. George Orwell *The Lion and the Unicorn (1941)*

On the increase in sports violence – These days playing fields *are* the Battle of Waterloo. Geraldine Bedell *Independent on Sunday* (1994)

The Battle of Waterloo is won by the first commuter to leap off an incoming train. Colin M. Jarman

❝ BEAT ❞

ANY STICK WILL BE FOUND TO BEAT A DOG.
T. BECON *WORKS* (1564)

Any stigma will do to beat a dogma. Philip Guedella

THEY SHALL BEAT THEIR SWORDS INTO PLOUGH-SHARES, AND THEIR SPEARS INTO PRUNING HOOKS.
ISAIAH 2:4 *THE BIBLE*

Some happy day we shall beat our swords into plowshares and our jazz bands into unconsciousness. *Baltimore Sun*

❝ BEAUTIFUL ❞

BLACK IS BEAUTIFUL.
STOKELY CARMICHAEL *SPEECH* (1966)

Black is beautiful, but unemployed. US Graffiti

SMALL IS BEAUTIFUL.
E. F. SCHUMACHER *BOOK TITLE* (1973)

Not only small but piecemeal is beautiful. *Country Life* (1975)

Small is beautiful – but big pays more. D. James *Spy at Evening* (1977)

" BEAUTY "

BEAUTY IS BUT SKIN DEEP.

JOHN DAVIES *A SELECT HUSBAND* (1616)

Beauty is only skin deep, but ugly goes clear to the bone.

A. B. Evans (1881)

Mother used to say that beauty was only skin deep, but I never before realised that bones could be so fearfully repulsive.

E. M. Ingraham *Bond and Free* (1882)

Beauty is only skin deep – but it's a valuable asset if you're poor and haven't any sense.   Kin Hubbard

The saying that beauty is but skin deep is but a skin deep saying.

Herbert Spencer

I always say beauty is only sin deep.   Saki (H. H. Munro)

It's a good thing that beauty is only skin deep, or I'd be rotten to the core.   Phyllis Diller

Beauty is only skin deep, and the world is full of thin-skinned people.

Richard Armour

Beauty is only skin-deep, but it's only the skin you see.

A. Price *'44 Vintage* (1978)

I'm tired of all this nonsense about beauty being only skin deep. That's deep enough. What do you want – an adorable pancreas?

Jean Kerr *The Snakes Has All the Lines*

Thanks to plastic surgery, beauty in Hollywood is skin tight.

Victoria Principal (1993)

Beauty is only skin deep, ugly lies the bone.
    Beauty dies and fades away, but ugly holds its own.   Anon

Nepotism is only kin deep.   Anon

BEAUTY IS IN THE EYE OF THE BEHOLDER.

MARGARET HUNGERFORD *MOLLY BROWN* (1878)

Competence, like truth, beauty and contact lenses, is in the eye of the beholder.   Laurence J. Peter *The Peter Principle*

The eyes of the beholders are so affected by their brains that they see not precisely what is before them, but what they wish to be there.

Geoffrey Squire *Dress and Society* (1972)

Logic is in the eye of the logician.   Gloria Steinem *The First Ms Reader* (1972)

It does not matter if beauty is in the eye of the beholder: you can always find out what the beholder likes.

J. R. Richards *Sceptical Feminist* (1980)

Pornography is in the groin of the beholder.   Charles Rembar

BEAUTY IS TRUTH – TRUTH BEAUTY.

JOHN KEATS *ODE TO A GRECIAN URN* (1819)

If truth is beauty, how come no one has their hair done in the library?

Lily Tomlin

A THING OF BEAUTY IS A JOY FOREVER.

JOHN KEATS *ENDYMION* (1818)

The question is, had he not been a thing of beauty,
Would she be swayed by quite so keen a sense of duty?

W. S. Gilbert *The Pirates of Penzance* (1879)

Somehow a bachelor never quite gets over the idea that he is a thing
of beauty and a boy forever.   Helen Rowland *A Guide to Men* (1922)

On the youthfulness of the Police Force – A thing of duty is a boy for
ever.   Flann O'Brien

A thing of beauty is a great expense.   Herbert V. Prochnow

A thing of beauty keeps you broke forever.   Anon

A garden is a thing of beauty and a job forever.   Anon

—————————— **❝ BED ❞** ——————————

AS YOU HAVE MADE YOUR BED, SO YOU MUST LIE IN IT.
PROVERB

There is a proverb, 'As you have made your bed, so you must lie in
it', which is simply a lie. If I have made my bed uncomfortable,
please God, I will make it again.   G. K. Chesterton

If you make your bed, you must lie in it, particularly if it is a
marriage-bed.   James Hilton (1933)

You have made your own hangover so you can groan in it.

Don Williams *From Hamstringing the Hangover* (1957)

EARLY TO BED AND EARLY TO RISE MAKES A MAN HEALTHY, WEALTHY AND WISE.
PROVERB

Early to bed and early to rise
Will make you miss all the regular guys.   George Ade (1900)

Early to bed and early to rise is a bad rule for anyone who wishes to
become acquainted with our most prominent and influential people.

George Ade

Early to rise and early to bed
Makes a male healthy, wealthy and dead.   James Thurber

Early to bed,
And you'll wish you were dead.
Bed before eleven,
Nuts before seven.   Dorothy Parker *The Little Hour* (1936)

Early to bed, and early to rise,
Work like hell, and advertise.   Laurence J. Peter

Early to bed and early to rise makes a man a big nuisance.
                                          Joseph Lazanoff

Early to rise and late to bed
Lifts again the debtor's head.   Anon

Late to bed and early to rise
Keeps a twinkle in the eyes.   Anon

Early to bed, and early to rise,
If you want your head to feel its normal size.   Anon

─────── **❝ BEDFELLOWS ❞** ───────

POVERTY MAKES STRANGE BEDFELLOWS.

ENGLISH PROVERB

Politics makes strange bedfellows.   Charles Dudly
Politics makes strange bedfellows rich.   Wayne Haisey

───────────── **❝ BEE ❞** ─────────────

AS BUSY AS A BEE.

GEOFFREY CHAUCER *THE MERCHANT'S TALE* (1386)

He is as busy as a bee with two tails.
                        John B. Ker *Popular English Phrases* (1834)

Bees are not as busy as we think they are. They just can't buzz any
    slower.   Kin Hubbard

It isn't so much how busy you are – but why you are busy. The bee is
    praised. The mosquito is swatted.   Roger Devlin

On Muhammad Ali (Boxer) – **HE FLOATS LIKE A
BUTTERFLY; STINGS LIKE A BEE,
YOUR HANDS CAN'T HIT WHAT YOUR EYES CAN'T
SEE.**   DREW 'BUNDINI' BROWN (c. 1964)

On Muhammad Ali – He stings like a bee, but lives like a W.A.S.P.
                                          Eamonn Andrews

On Muhammad Ali – At 39, Ali floats like an anchor, and stings like a moth.
Ray Gandolf

On Trevor Brooking (Football player) – He floats like a butterfly, and stings like one, too.
Brian Clough

On Martin Offiah (Rugby player) – Your hands can't CATCH what your eyes can't see.
Nike rugby boot advert (1993)

❝ BEGGARS ❞

BEGGARS CAN'T BE CHOOSERS.
JOHN HEYWOOD PROVERBS (1546)

Buggers can't be choosers.
Maurice Bowra

Beggars are never losers.
L. L. Levinson

Burghers count beach-users.
Denis Nordern My Word (1978)

On Keith Chegwin – Cheggers can't be boozers.
Colin M. Jarman

❝ BEHIND ❞

BEHIND EVERY SUCCESSFUL MAN STANDS A WOMAN.
CHINESE PROVERB

We in the movie industry know that behind every successful screenwriter stands a woman. And behind that woman is his wife.
Groucho Marx

Behind every successful man, you'll find a woman who has nothing to wear.
James Stewart

Behind every successful man, there's a very surprised mother-in-law.
Hubert H. Humphrey Speech (1964)

Behind every successful decathlete stands a good doctor.
Bill Toomey (1968)

Behind almost every woman you ever heard stands a man who let her down.
Naomi Bliven

On Yoko Ono – As usual there is a great woman behind every idiot.
John Lennon

Behind every successful businesswoman is a man without a chip on his shoulder.
Richard Ross (1989)

Behind every successful man is a good woman – an exhausted one.
Sarah Ferguson

Behind every world class goalkeeper there's a ball from Ian Wright.
Nike football boot advert (1993)

Behind every successful man, there's a woman who couldn't be more
    surprised.   Anon

Behind every successful man, there's a woman telling him that he isn't
    so hot.   Anon

Behind every successful man, there's a woman who keeps reminding
    him that she knows someone who would have done it better.   Anon

Behind every successful man, there's a woman after his job.   Anon

Behind every successful man is a fish with a bicycle.   Graffiti

—————— ❝ BELIEVING ❞ ——————

SEEING IS BELIEVING.   M. HAYWARD (1609)

Seeing is deceiving. It's eating that's believing.   James Thurber

Some things have got to be be believed to be seen.   Ralph Hodgson

Hurtling down an icy slope, 'round icy hummocks weaving' –
Such enthusiasm can only attest that skiing is believing. George O. Ludcke

Being is believing.   Anon

Peeing is relieving.   Colin M. Jarman

——————— ❝ BEST ❞ ———————

THE BEST YEARS OF OUR LIVES.   FILM TITLE (1946)

On Clark Gable (Actor) – He has the best ears of our lives.   Milton Berle

After the 1990 Football World Cup Finals – Paul Gascoigne revealed
    the best tears of our lives.   Colin M. Jarman *Roy of the Rovers*

——————— ❝ BETTER ❞ ———————

BETTER RED THAN DEAD.   ANTI-NUCLEAR SLOGAN

Better dead than Red.   Anti-Communist slogan

Better wed than dead.   *Love with a Proper Stranger* (1974)

Better dead than read.   'Bookworm' *Private Eye* (1994)

THE BETTER PART OF VALOUR IS DISCRETION
                WILLIAM SHAKESPEARE *HENRY IV PT 1* (1597)

Discretion is not the better part of biography.   Lytton Strachey

Desertion is the better part of valour.   American Saying

Digestion is the better part of à la carte.   Anon

FOR BETTER OR FOR WORSE, FOR RICHER OR FOR POORER.
THE BOOK OF COMMON PRAYER (1662)

On her husband's retirement – I married George for better or for
worse, but not for lunch.
Hazel Weiss (1960)

Hollywood is a place where a woman takes a man for better or for
worse, but not for keeps.
Anon

'TIS BETTER TO HAVE LOVED AND LOST, THAN NEVER TO HAVE LOVED AT ALL.
ALFRED, LORD TENNYSON *IN MEMORIAM* (1850)

'Tis better to have fought and lost, than never to have fought at all.
Arthur Hugh Clough *Peschiera*

'Tis better to have loved and lost, than never to have lost at all.
Samuel Butler *The Way of All Flesh* (1903)

It is better to have loafed and lost than never to have loafed at all.
James Thurber *Father for our Time*

Far better to have loved and lost than to be buying shoes for eight
kids.
William Walton

It is better to have loved your wife than never to have loved at all.
Edgar Saltus

Better to have loved and lost a short person than never to have loved
a tall.
David Chambless

In politics, it is better never to have loved at all than to haved loved
and lost.
G. Lyall *Secret Servant* (1980)

It is better to have loved and lost, than to have paid for it and not
liked it.
Graffiti

Better to have loved and lost than to have spent your whole life with
him.
Graffiti

—————— **" BIRD "** ——————

A BIRD IN THE HAND IS WORTH TWO IN THE BUSH.
AESOP *FABLES* (750 BC)

A hair in the head is worth two in the brush.
Oliver Herford

Ecology is the belief that a bird in the bush is worth two in the hand.
Stanley C. Gibbons

A bird in bed is worth two in the bushes.
Lambert Jeffries

A bird in the hand is a positive embarrassment to one not in the
poultry business.
George Ade *Fables*

A bird in the hand is bad table manners.
L. L. Levinson

A ring on the finger is worth two on the phone.   Harold W. Thompson

A bird in the hand is worth two in Shepherd's Bush.   *Minder* – ITV series

A girl in the bed is worth two in the car.   American Saying

A bird in the hand is usually dead.   Anon

A bird in the hand does it on your wrist.   Graffiti

An orgasm in the bush is worth two in the hand.   Graffiti

THE EARLY BIRD CATCHES THE WORM.

WILLIAM CAMDEN *RECOLLECTIONS* (1636)

The early tire gets the roofin' tack.   Elbert Hubbard

The early bird catches the worm – unfortunately, it is the early fish
that catches the worm. But the early man catches the fish.

G. K. Chesterton *Fad of the Fisherman* (1922)

She was one of the early birds and I was one of the worms. T. W. Connor

The early bird wishes he'd let someone else get up first.   Mrs A. Simmons

Never be a pioneer. It's the early Christian that gets the fattest lion.

Saki

The early bird gathers no moss.   Nat West Bank small business advert (1991)

The early bird gets the late one's breakfast.   Anon

The early worm gets caught.   Anon

If the early bird gets the worm, my advice for worms is to sleep late.

Anon

HE THINKS TO KILL TWO BIRDS WITH ONE STONE, AND SATISFY TWO ARGUMENTS WITH ONE ANSWER.

THOMAS HOBBES (1656)

Three birds with one stone is quite good marksmanship.

J. J. Connington *No Past is Dead* (1942)

An efficiency expert is a man who kills two birds with one stone – and
gets the stone back.   Anon

A Christmas turkey is a good way to put on two stone from one bird.

Anon

❝ BITE ❞

BITE OFF MORE THAN YOU CAN CHEW.   ANON SAYING

The moral is you know your biz when the pie is passed by fate,
And not to indulge in a larger bite, than you can masticate.

J. Cheever Goodwin *Wang* (1891)

On novelist Henry James – It's not that he bites off more than he can
  chew but he chews more than he bites off.   Clover Adams

Bite off only what you can chew easily. It tastes better that way – any
  epicure can tell you that.   D. H. Fink *Release from Nervous Tension* (1943)

On Robert Kennedy – That was the Kennedy way: you bit off more
  than you could chew and then you chewed it.   Gerald Gardner

Do not write off more than you can eschew.   Denis Nordern *My Word* (1980)

HE IS WONDERFULLY UNLUCKY, INSOMUCH THAT HE WILL BITE THE HAND THAT FEEDS HIM.

JOSEPH ADDISON *SPECTATOR* (1711)

A film director is a person who bites the hen that lays the golden egg.
                                                          Samuel Goldwyn

There are times when parenthood seems nothing but feeding the
  mouth that bites you.   Peter de Vries

A mosquito bites the hand that feeds it.   *Financial America*

People who bite the hands that feeds them, usually lick the boot that
  kicks them.   Eric Hoffer

The noblest of all dogs is the hot-dog: it feeds the hand that bites it.
                                                         Laurence J. Peter

Never bite the hands that feeds you canapés.
                                            Kent Woking *The Guardian* (1993)

An actor's agent is a guy who sometimes bites the ham that feeds him.
                                                                    Anon

—————— **❝ BLESSED ❞** ——————

BLESSED ARE THE PEACEMAKERS; FOR THEY SHALL BE CALLED THE CHILDREN OF GOD.

MATTHEW 5:9 *THE BIBLE*

Cursed are the peacemakers.   Rolf Hochhuth *The Representatives*

Blessed are the cheesemakers.   *Monty Python's Life of Brian* (1979)

Blessed are the peacemakers, for they will never be unemployed.   Anon

BLESSED ARE THE PURE IN HEART: FOR THEY SHALL SEE GOD.   MATTHEW 5:8 *THE BIBLE*

Blessed are the pure in heart for they have so much more to talk
  about.   Edith Wharton *John O'London's Weekly* (1932)

Blessed are the pure in art.   Anon

I HAVE A NINTH BEATITUDE . . . BLESSED IS HE WHO EXPECTS NOTHING, FOR HE SHALL NEVER BE DISAPPOINTED.   ALEXANDER POPE *LETTER* (1725)

Blessed is he who expecteth nothing, for he shall be gloriously
    surprised.   G. K. Chesterton

IT IS MORE BLESSED TO GIVE THAN TO RECEIVE.
                                    ACTS OF THE APOSTLES 20:35 *THE BIBLE*

It's better to give than to lend, and it doesn't cost any more.
                                                          Sir Phillip Gibbs

'Tis more blessed to give than receive, for example, wedding presents.
                                                           H. L. Mencken

It is certainly more agreeable to have power to give than receive.
                                                        Sir Winston Churchill

It's more blessed to give than to receive – especially kittens.   Bill Cosby

It is more blessed to give than receive – and it is often tax deductible.
                                                                    Anon

Experience the joys of giving and receiving – masturbate. American Graffiti

—————— " BLIND " ——————

AMONG THE BLIND, THE ONE-EYED MAN IS KING.
                                                        ERASMUS (c 1500)

In the country of the blind, the one-eyed person is a beauty.
                                                          Arabic Proverb

In the country of the blind, the one-eyed king can still goof up.
                                                        Laurence J. Peter

On Shere Hite (Feminist author) – In the land of the blind, one idea is
    all you need to be a queen.   *Observer* (1994)

IF THE BLIND SHALL LEAD THE BLIND, BOTH SHALL FALL INTO THE DITCH.   MATTHEW 15:14 *THE BIBLE*

When the blind lead the blind they both fall into matrimony.
                                    George Farquhar *Love and a Bottle* (1698)

The young leading the young is like the blind leading the blind.
                                            Lord Chesterfield *Letter* (1747)

An Englishman teaching an American about food is like the blind
    leading the one-eyed.   A. J. Liebling

The blind lead the blind. It's the democratic way.
                            Henry Miller *The Air-Conditioned Nightmare* (1945)

Television is the bland leading the bland.
                    Murray Schumach *The Face on the Cutting Room Floor* (1964)

BETTER . . . THAN . . .

Better a certain enemy than a doubtful friend
Aesop The Hound and the Hare (570 BC)

Better a snotty child than his nose wiped off.
Randall Cotgrave French and English Tongue (1611)

Better be the head of an ass than the tail of a horse.
John Clarke Anglo-Latina (1639)

Better be out of the world than out of the fashion. *John Clarke Ibid.* (1639)

Better to go to heaven in rags than to hell in embroidery.
Thomas Fuller Gnomologia (1732)

Better a lean compromise than a fat lawsuit.
George Herbert Outlandish Proverbs (1640)

Better to die on your feet than to live on your knees.
Dolores Ibarruri (1936)

Better sleep with a sober cannibal than a drunken Christian.
Herman Melville Moby Dick (1851)

Better a bald head than none at all. *Austin O'Malley*

Better by far you should forget and smile than you should remember
and be sad. *Christina Rossetti Remember* (1862)

Better a witty fool than a foolish wit. *William Shakespeare Twelfth Night*

Better stay up all night than go to bed with a dragon.
Jeremy Taylor (1650)

Better to be thought a fool than open your mouth and prove it.
Bob Turnell (1987)

Better to trip in with the feet than with the tongue. *Zeno* (300 BC)

Better a red face than a black heart. *Portuguese Proverb*

Better a quiet death than a public misfortune. *Spanish Proverb*

Better to be a has-been than a never was. *American Saying*

Better to split hairs than split heads. *American Saying*

Better red wine than red blood. *Anon*

❝ BODY ❞

LEAVE YOUR BODY TO SCIENCE. ANON

He left his body to science – and science is contesting the will.
David Frost

When I die, I am going to leave my body to science fiction. Steve Wright

"BORN"

EVERY MAN IS NOT BORN WITH A SILVER SPOON IN HIS MOUTH.
MIGUEL DE CERVANTES *DON QUIXOTE* (1615)

One man is born with a silver spoon in his mouth, another with a
wooden ladle.
Oliver Goldsmith (1762)

They who are born with silver spoons in their mouths, don't know
how to use them.
W. C. Hazlitt (1869)

He was born with a knife, a fork and a spoon in his mouth.
Ring Lardner *Horseshoes* (1926)

It was said he was born with a white tie in his mouth.
Christopher Hale *Rumour Hath It* (1945)

I was born with a plastic spoon in my mouth.
Peter Townshend *Substitute* (1966)

On Malcolm Fraser (Australian Premier) – He is the cutlery man of
Australia. He was born with a silver spoon in his mouth, speaks
with a forked tongue and knifes his colleagues in the back.
Bob Hawke (1975)

On Christopher Martin-Jenkins (Radio 3 cricket commentator) – Born
with a diamond-encrusted golden spoon thrust well down the
throat.
Don Mosey *The Alderman's Tale* (1991)

I AM NATIVE HERE, AND TO THE MANOR BORN.
WILLIAM SHAKESPEARE *HAMLET* (1602)

He ordered as one to the menu born.
O. Henry

Democrats are to the manna born.
Ogden Nash

All of us are to the manners born.
Duke of Devonshire (1993)

MAN IS BORN FREE AND EVERYWHERE HE IS IN CHAINS.
JEAN-JACQUES ROUSSEAU *DU CONTRAT SOCIAL* (1672)

Man is not born free; he is born attached to his mother by a cord and
is incapable of looking after himself for at least seven years.
Katherine Whitehorn

All men are born free and unequal.
Grant Allen

All men are born free, but some get married.
Anon

All men are born free except at a private maternity hospital.
Anon

Man is born free but everywhere is in chains. Smash the cistern.
Graffiti

SOME MEN ARE BORN GREAT, SOME ACHIEVE GREATNESS, AND SOME HAVE GREATNESS THRUST UPON THEM.
WILLIAM SHAKESPEARE *TWELFTH NIGHT* (1600)

My time has not yet come either; some men are born posthumously.
Friedrich Nietzsche *Ecce Homo* (1888)

Some men are born great, some achieve greatness and others just keep still.
Kin Hubbard

Some people are born with a sense of how to clothe themselves, others acquire it, others look as if their clothes had been thrust upon them.
Saki

Some men are born great, some achieve greatness, and others thrust greatness upon themselves.
Boston Post

Some men are born great, some achieve greatness, and some hire public relations officers.
Daniel J. Boorstin

Some men are born mediocre, some men achieve mediocrity, and some men have mediocrity thrust upon them. With Major Major it has been all three.
Joseph Heller *Catch 22*

Some are born lazy, some have idleness thrust upon them and others spend a great deal of effort creating a careless nonchalance.
Beryl Downing *The Times* (1980)

Some people are born great, some achieve greatness, and some just grate.
Anon

❝ BOW ❞

I WILL WELL THAT EVERY MAN BE AMOROUS AND LOVE, BUT THAT HE HAVE TWO STRINGS TO HIS BOW. WILLIAM CAXTON *THE HISTORY OF JASON* (1477)

Some women feel more secure with a second string to their bow. I like it when I have a second beau on my string.
E. S. Gardner (1943)

❝ BOY ❞

BOYS WILL BE BOYS. ANON SAYING

Girls will be girls. They like admiration.
William M. Thackeray *Vanity Fair* (1847)

Boys will be boys – and even that . . . wouldn't matter if we could only prevent girls from being girls. Anthony Hope *The Dolly Dialogues* (1894)

Boys will be boys, and so will a lot of middle-aged men. Kin Hubbard

Boys will be boys these days, and so apparently will girls. Jane Howard

**THE BOY STOOD ON THE BURNING DECK,
WHENCE ALL BUT HE HAD FLED;
THE FLAME THAT LIT THE BATTLE'S WRECK
SHONE ROUND HIM O'ER THE DEAD.**

FELICIA HEMANS *CASABIANCA* (1829)

The boy stood on the burning deck,
His feet were covered with blisters.
He had no trousers of his own
And so he wore his sister's.   Anon

The boy stood on the burning deck,
The flame around him flickers,
He said, *It doesn't bother me,
I've got asbestos knickers!*   Anon

❝ BRAVE ❞

NONE BUT THE BRAVE DESERVE THE FAIR.

JOHN DRYDEN *ALEXANDER'S FEAST* (1697)

None but the brave desert the fair.   Addison Mizner

None but the brave can live with the fair.   Elbert Hubbard

Only the brave chemin de fer.   Robert E. Sherwood

Only the brave deserve the fair, but only the rich, fat and cowardly
merchants can afford the same.   Anon

After an increase in bus fares – None but the brave deserve the fare.

Graffiti (1980)

❝ BREAD ❞

CAST THY BREAD UPON THE WATERS: FOR THOU SHALT FIND IT AFTER MANY DAYS.

ECCLESIASTES 11:1 *THE BIBLE*

Cast thy bread upon the waters and it will come back to you –
buttered.   Elbert Hubbard (1911)

On recruiting dancers from a showboat – I bred my cast upon the
waters.   Ed Wynn (1940)

I cast my bread upon the water and I got back a bakery shop.

Catherine Cookson (1974)

Cast your bed upon the waters and you shall have wet dreams.   Anon

---

❝ BRIDGE ❞

DON'T BURN YOUR BRIDGES.
ANON SAYING

He burned his bridges while they were changing horses in midstream.
Stanley Walker *New Yorker* (1941)

Never burn your bridges till you come to them.   Clayton Rawson (1942)

A politician is a man who burns his bridges before he comes to them.
Leonid Brezhnev

When one burns one's bridges, what a very nice fire it makes.
Dylan Thomas

A pessimist is a person who burns his bridges before he comes to
them.   Anon

DON'T CROSS A BRIDGE TILL YOU COME TO IT.
PROVERB (c. 1700)

We can't cross a bridge until we come to it, but I always like to lay
down a pontoon ahead of time.   Bernard Baruch

A politician is a person who will double-cross a bridge when he comes
to it.   Oscar Levant

Don't cross your bridges till you've burned them.   Dick Bower

Don't cross your bridge till you come to it, and then be sure there's a
bridge.   Anon

❝ BULL ❞

TAKE THE BULL BY THE HORNS.
SPANISH PROVERB

You ought to take the bull by the teeth.   Samuel Goldwyn

When you take the bull by the horns . . . what happens is a toss-up.
William P. Ridge

She has got to take her nerve by the horns.   Virginia Wade

Someone in the England [football] team has to take the ball by the
horns.   Ron Atkinson (1993)

Our members will be grasping the bull by the horns only to find that
it's a damp squib.   Anon T.U.C. Member

During the bad times we bit the bull by the horns.   Nate Rosenblatt

" BUSINESS "

THERE'S NO BUSINESS LIKE SHOW BUSINESS.

IRVING BERLIN *SONG TITLE* (1946)

No biz like faux biz. *Variety*

There's no business like show business – except sports business.

William J. Baker

On David Mellor's affair with Antonia de Sancha – There's no business like toe business. *Private Eye* (1994)

" BUTTER "

HE MADE AS THOUGH BUTTER WOULD NOT MELT IN HIS MOUTH. JOHN PALSGRAVE (1530)

She looks as though butter wouldn't melt in her mouth but, I warrant, cheese won't choke her. Jonathan Swift *Polite Conversations* (1738)

On Maureen O'Hara (Actress) – She looked as though butter wouldn't melt in her mouth – or anywhere else for that matter.

Elsa Lanchester

" CAKE "

LET THEM EAT CAKE! MARIE-ANTOINETTE Attrib.

Marie-Antoinette made only one mistake. She should have said, 'Let them eat hokum'. Westbrook Pegler *Fair Enough* (1934)

Let them drink Coke. Colin M. Jarman

YOU CAN'T HAVE YOUR CAKE AND EAT IT. PROVERB

We can't have archaic, and eat it too. Dorothy Parker

I hope, before I'm through
To have my cake and bake it too. Margaret Fishback *Career Girl*

You can't advocate and eat at two. Denis Nordern *My Word* (1978)

You can have your cake and eat it, the only trouble is you get fat.

Julian Barnes *Flaubert's Parrot* (1984)

" CALL "

THE POT CALLING THE KETTLE BLACK. SAYING

On Lord Hill's autobiography – Like the slag-heap calling a polar bear black.   Bernard Levin *Observer* (1974)

On Dr David Owen backing the Conservative Party in the 1992 General Election – A case of the doc calling the kettle black.
                                                          Jane Gordon *Today* (1992)

A modern kitchen is where the pot calls the kettle chartreuse.   Anon

—————— 66 CAME 99 ——————

VENI, VIDI, VICI *(I came, I saw, I conquered).*   Julius Caesar

After his victory over the Turks – I came, I saw; God conquered.
                                                          King John III of Poland

Veni, vidi, visa – We came, we saw, we shopped.   Jan Barrett

Veni, vidi, video – We came, we saw, we filmed.
                                                          John Naughton *Observer* (1993)

Veni, vidi, wiwi – We came, we saw, we pissed ourselves.   Graffiti

Vidi, vici, veni – We saw, we conquered, we came.   Graffiti

—————— 66 CAN 99 ——————

HE WHO CAN, DOES. HE WHO CANNOT, TEACHES.
                                                          G. B. SHAW *MAN AND SUPERMAN* (1902)

Those who can, act. Those who can't, teach. And those who can't do either, review.   Burt Reynolds

Film directors who can, do. Directors who can't, parody.
                                                          Robert Leedham *The Guardian* (1993)

When it comes to sex, those who can, do, those who can't, date.
                                                          Julie Burchill *Absolute Filth* (1993)

Women who can, do. Those who cannot, become feminists.   Anon

—————— 66 CANDY 99 ——————

CANDY IS DANDY, BUT LIQUOR IS QUICKER.
                                                          OGDEN NASH

Candy is dandy, but depravities won't give you cavities.   L. L. Levinson

On 'Candy' (1968) – As an emetic, liquor is dandy, but *Candy* is quicker.   John Simon

" CAN'T "

IF YOU CAN'T BEAT 'EM, JOIN 'EM.

AMERICAN POLITICAL MAXIM

If you can't beat 'em, confuse em. Harry S Truman

If you can't blind 'em with science, baffle 'em with bullshit.

Anon *Universal law of Bullshit*

" CARE "

TAKE CARE OF THE PENCE, AND THE POUNDS WILL TAKE CARE OF THEMSELVES. WILLIAM LOWNDES (c. 1720)

I recommend you to take care of the minutes; for the hours will look
after themselves. Lord Philip Chesterfield *Letter* (1747)

Take care of the sense, and the sounds will take care of themselves.

Lewis Carroll *Alice's Adventures in Wonderland* (1865)

If we take care of the actors the plays will take care of themselves.

G. B. Shaw (1913)

" CASTLE "

ALAS, ALL THE CASTLES I HAVE ARE BUILT WITH AIR. BEN JONSON *EASTWARD HOE!* (1604)

Castles in the air are very impregnable. Thomas Randolph (1651)

Castles in the air cost a vast deal to keep them up.

Edward Bulwer-Lytton (1838)

The are no rules of architecture for castles built in the air.

G. K. Chesterton

Castles in the air are the only property you can own without the
intervention of lawyers. Unfortunately, however, there are no title
deeds to them. J. Tudor Rees

Neurotics build castles in the air. Psychotics live in them. Psychiatrists
collect the rent. Lord Webb *Look* (1955)

(*Alan Hull added* . . . and psychopaths smash in the windows.)

Castles in the air are great, but try cutting the lawn. Anon

AN ENGLISHMAN'S HOME IS HIS CASTLE.

R. MULCASTER *POSITIONS* (1581)

Today nobody's house is his castle – it's a potential TV studio. T. S. Eliot

An Englishman's home is his tax haven. *The Economist*

An Englishman's home is his hassle. Paul D. Arnold

An Englishman's home is his council house.
Geraldine Bedell *Independent on Sunday* (1994)

An Englishman's home is his building society's. Anon

An Englishman's home is his castle – so go on, let him clean it.
Feminist Graffiti

❝ CAT ❞

I FORGOT I WAS LETTING THE CAT OUT OF THE BAG AGAIN. MARIA EDGEWORTH *THE PARENT'S ASSISTANT* (1796–1800)

Don't let the cat out of the bag after the barn door is locked.
Honey Flexer

Just enough points on the table for Tony Knowles to pull the cat out of the fire. Ray Edmonds (TV snooker commentator)

Gossip is the art of letting the chat out of the bag. Anon

WHILE THE CAT'S AWAY, THE MICE WILL PLAY.
SCOTTISH PROVERB

While the cat's away – there's less hair on the furniture. Robert Orben

While the cast is away, the understudies will play. Colin M. Jarman

❝ CAUSE ❞

I AM NOT ONLY WITTY IN MYSELF, BUT THE CAUSE THAT IS IN OTHER MEN.
WILLIAM SHAKESPEARE *HENRY IV Pt 2* (1591)

On Thomas Boswell (Samuel Johnson's biographer) – He is not only dull in himself, but the cause of dullness in others. Samuel Foote

❝ CHARITY ❞

CHARITY SHOULD BEGIN AT HOME. JOHN WYCLIF (1383)

Charity and beating begins at home.
Francis Beaumont and John Fletcher *Wit Without Money* (1616)

Charity begins at home, and justice begins next door.
Charles Dickens *Martin Chuzzlewit* (1843–4)

Charity begins at home, and usually stays there.   Elbert Hubbard

On James M. Whistler (painter) – With our James vulgarity begins at
home, and should be allowed to stay there.   Oscar Wilde

Censorship, like charity, should begin at home, but unlike charity, it
should end there.   Clare Booth Luce

On F. Scott Fitzgerald (author) – Mr Fitzgerald believes that plagiarism begins at home.   Zelda Fitzgerald

I prefer charity to hospitality because charity begins at home and
hospitality ends there.   Ogden Nash *I'll Stay Out Of Your Diet* (1942)

Charity begins at home, and usually ends up in some foreign country.
                    Anon

CHARITY SHALL COVER THE MULTITUDE OF SINS.

PETER 4:8 *THE BIBLE*

Charity creates a multitude of sins.   Oscar Wilde

Martyrdom covers a multitude of sins.   Mark Twain

Epigrams cover a multitude of sins.   Carolyn Wells

Charity uncovers a multitude of sins.   Carolyn Wells

You can say what you like about long dresses, but they cover a
multitude of shins.   Mae West *Peel Me a Grape*

❝ CHILD ❞

IT IS A WISE CHILD THAT KNOWS ITS OWN FATHER.

HOMER (c. 800 BC)

It is a wise father that knows his own child.
                    William Shakespeare *The Merchant of Venice* (1596)

It's a wise child that owes its own father.   Carolyn Wells

It's a wise child that knows its fodder.   Ogden Nash (1933)

It is a dull child that knows its own father.   Anon

❝ CHILDREN ❞

CHILDREN SHOULD BE SEEN AND NOT HEARD.

ARISTOPHANES (423 BC)

Whenever a child can be seen but not heard, it's a shame to wake him.
                    Hal Chadwick

Children should be serene and not scared.   R. I. Kimmons

Virgins should be seen more than they're heard.
Thomas Middleton *More Dissemblers Besides Women* (1622)

Fathers should be neither seen nor heard. That is the only proper basis for family life.
Oscar Wilde *An Ideal Husband* (1895)

On George Bernard Shaw – It is disappointing to report that George Bernard Shaw appearing as George Bernard Shaw is sadly miscast in the part. Satirists should be heard and not seen. Robert E. Sherwood

On the advent of 'talking' movies – I am convinced that films should be seen and not heard.
Ernest Betts

On author Truman Capote – He should be heard, and not read.
Gore Vidal

Writers should be read – but neither seen nor heard. Daphne du Maurier

Women should be obscene and not heard. John Lennon

Music should be heard and not seen. Sony Mini Hi-Fi Advert

Children should be seen and not hurt. Texaco Road Safety Slogan

Every little bean must be heard as well as seen. Anon

Soup should be seen and not heard. Anon

Collectively, geese should be skein and not herd. Colin M. Jarman

—————————— ❝ CHIP ❞ ——————————

HE'S A CHIP OF THE OLD BLOCK. WILLIAM ROWLEY (1633)

She's a chick of the old cock. Aphra Behn (1678)

On William Pitt the Younger (Prime Minister) – Not merely a chip of the old block, but the old block itself. Edmund Burke (1781)

A PROVOCATION TO A FIGHT IS PLACING A CHIP UPON A MAN'S SHOULDER AND DARING ANOTHER TO KNOCK IT OFF. HARPER'S MAGAZINE (1857)

Don't let that chip on your shoulder be your only reason for walking erect. James Thurber *Midnight at Tim's Place* (1961)

On singer Billy Joel – Perfectly balanced. Chips on both shoulders.
Q magazine (1986)

❝ CHIPS ❞

GOODBYE, MR CHIPS. JAMES HILTON *BOOK TITLE* (1934)
Good pie, missed the chips. Frank Muir *My Word* (1974)

❝ CHOSEN ❞

FOR MANY ARE CALLED BUT FEW ARE CHOSEN.
MATTHEW *THE BIBLE*
Many are cold, but few are frozen. Frank Muir *My Word* (1980)

❝ CHRISTMAS ❞

CHRISTMAS COMES BUT ONCE A YEAR.
THOMAS TUSSER *FIVE HUNDRED POINTS OF GOOD HUSBANDRY* (1557)
Father Christmas comes once a year – what a pity. Mae West
Christmas comes, but once a year is enough. Anon

❝ CIRCUMVENT ❞

A BAD POLITICIAN IS ONE THAT WOULD CIRCUM-VENT GOD. WILLIAM SHAKESPEARE *HAMLET* (1602)
A good lawyer is one who would circumvent the law. Ambrose Bierce

❝ CITY ❞

OXFORD – AND THAT SWEET CITY WITH HER DREAMING SPIRES. MATTHEW ARNOLD *THYRSIS* (1866)

Oxford – city of expiring dreams.   *Isis Magazine* (1970s)
Cambridge – this is the city of perspiring dreams.

Frederic Raphael *The Glittering Prizes*

PHILADELPHIA IS THE CITY OF BROTHERLY LOVE.

ANON

New York is the city of brotherly shove.   Anon

A TALE OF TWO CITIES.   CHARLES DICKENS *BOOK TITLE* (1859)

On Oxford and Cambridge – A tale of two varsities.

Michael Durham *Observer* (1993)

On actress Raquel Welch – A tale of two titties.   Anon

——————— **" CLASSES "** ———————

SOCIETY IS DIVIDED INTO TWO CLASSES: THE SHEARERS AND THE SHORN.   CHARLES M. DE TALLEYRAND

Society is composed of two great classes: those who have more dinners than appetite, and those who have more appetite than dinners.

Nicholas de Chamfort

There are three classes of elderly women; first, that dear old soul; second, that old woman; third, that old witch.   Samuel Taylor Coleridge

Three classes of clergy: Nimrods, Ramrods and fishing rods.

Vincent Lean (1904)

There are only two classes in good society in England: the equestrian classes and the neurotic classes.   George Bernard Shaw

There are only two classes – first class and no class.   David O. Selznick

In America, there are two classes of travel – first class, and with children.   Robert Benchley

Hats generally divide into three classes: offensive hats, defensive hats, and shrapnel.   Katherine Whitehorn

Widows are divided into two classes – the bereaved and the relieved.

Anon

There are three classes of man in the United States: the intellectual, the handsome and the majority.   Anon

❝ CLEANLINESS ❞

CLEANLINESS IS INDEED NEXT TO GODLINESS.
JOHN WESLEY *SERMONS ON DRESS* (1780)

Cleanliness is almost as bad as godliness.   Samuel Butler

They say cleanliness is next to godliness . . . I say it is next to impossible.   Edward Streeter *Dear Mabel* (1918)

Homeliness, not cleanliness, is next to godliness.
Victor Lewis-Smith *Evening Standard* (1994)

Cleanliness is next to godliness, only in an Irish dictionary.   Anon

Cleanliness may be next to godliness, but it is not a substitute.   Anon

Cleanliness may have been next to godliness, but both tenants vacated some years ago.   Anon

❝ CLOSED ❞

A CLOSED MOUTH CATCHES NO FLIES.   ITALIAN PROVERB

A closed ear catches no lies.   L. L. Levinson

A closed mouth gathers no feet.   Anon

❝ CLOTHES ❞

MANNERS AND CLOTHES MAKE THE MAN.
ANON SAYING (c. 1350)

Dress does not make the man, but it often makes a successful one.
Benjamin Disraeli *Endymion* (1880)

Clothes and manners do not make the man; but, when he is made, they greatly improve his appearance.   Henry W. Beecher (1887)

Manners maketh man – yes, but they make women still more.
Samuel Butler *Notebooks* (1912)

Clothes don't make the man, but they help a lot as far as businessmen are concerned.   Thomas J. Watson Jr.

Clothes don't make a man, but they break a husband.   Anon

Clothes do not make a man – especially an apron.   Anon

" CLOTHING "

BEWARE OF THE WOLF IN SHEEP'S CLOTHING.
AESOP (800 BC)

The Russians seemed to me a nation of sheep – angry sheep, but nevertheless sheep, and in sheep's clothing.
James Kirkup *One Man's Russia* (1968)

Far from being a loony left wolf in sheep's clothing, Paul Boateng comes across as a sheep who used to dress in wolf's clothing to keep up with the fashions. Joe Joseph *The Times* (1992)

Beware of the wolf in cheap clothing. Anon

" CLOUD "

I WANDERED LONELY AS A CLOUD.
THAT FLOATS ON HIGH O'ER VALES AND HILLS,
WHEN ALL AT ONCE I SAW A CROWD,
A HOST, OF GOLDEN DAFFODILS.
WILLIAM WORDSWORTH 'DAFFODILS' (1804)

On The Lake District – I wandered lonely as a cloud – through a horde of tourists. *Daily Mail* (1993)

I wandered lonely as a cloud – because I had B.O. Graffiti

EVERY CLOUD HAS A SILVER LINING.
JOHN MILTON *COMUS* (1634)

Every crowd has a silver lining. P. T. Barnum

Disobedience is the silver lining in the cloud of servitude.
Ambrose Bierce (1906)

My clouds have at least pewter linings. Ilka Chase *Past Imperfect* (1942)

Every cloud has a silver lining, but it is sometimes a little difficult to get it to the mint. Don Marquis

Every silver lining has its dark cloud. Sheila Levinson

On economic cutbacks – There's always the cloud with the silver lining, though we may well have to sell the silver lining. Harry Secombe (1974)

Every cloud has a silver lining and even an old suit of clothes has its shiny side. Anon

❝ COALS ❞

SALT TO DYSART, OR COALS TO NEWCASTLE.
SIR JAMES MELVILLE (1583)

On Sir Samuel Hoare [Foreign Secretary] – No more coals to Newcastle, no more Hoares to Paris.
King George V

❝ COMEDY ❞

THE COMEDY OF ERRORS.
WILLIAM SHAKESPEARE *PLAY TITLE* (c. 1594)

Love is the Comedy of Eros.
Evan Esar

❝ COMMITTEE ❞

A COMMITTEE IS A GROUP OF THE UNWILLING, PICKED FROM THE UNFIT, TO DO THE UNNECESSARY.
RICHARD HARKNESS *NEW YORK HERALD TRIBUNE* (1960)

We are the unwilling, led by the unqualified, doing the unnecessary for the ungrateful.
US Army Slogan in Vietnam

❝ COMPANY ❞

TWO'S COMPANY, THREE'S A CROWD.
PROVERB

You don't seem to realise, that in married life, three is company and two is none.
Oscar Wilde *The Importance of Being Earnest* (1895)

Two's company, three's a chaperon.
Philip Moeller *Madame San* (1917)

One's company, two's a crowd, and three's a party.
Andy Warhol

Three is company – two is merely compromising.
Frank Richardson

Two's company, three's a party, but four's a dinner party.
Julie Burchill *Absolute Filth* (1993)

Two is company, three is grounds for divorce.
Bill Cosby *You Bet Your Life* (1993)

Two is company. Three is the result.
Anon

Two's company policy, three is a takeover bid.
Anon

Two's company, three is troilism.
Anon

CORRUPTS

UNLIMITED POWER IS APT TO CORRUPT THE MINDS OF THOSE WHO POSSESS IT.
WILLIAM PITT THE ELDER

Power corrupts, but lack of power corrupts absolutely.
Adlai Stevenson

All power corrupts, and horse-power corrupts absolutely.
John Hillaby

Powerlessness corrupts. Absolute powerlessness corrupts absolutely.
Rosabeth Kantor

Leisure tends to corrupt. Absolute leisure corrupts absolutely.
Edgar Shoaff

Power dements even more than it corrupts.
W. and A. Durant

If absolute power corrupts absolutely where does this leave God?
George Deacon

COUNTED

STAND UP AND BE COUNTED.
ANON SAYING

It's time to lie down and be counted.
Mixmaster Morris (1993)

COUNTRY

AND SO, MY FELLOW AMERICANS, ASK NOT WHAT YOUR COUNTRY CAN DO FOR YOU; ASK WHAT YOU CAN DO FOR IT.
JOHN F. KENNEDY *SPEECH* (1961)

Ask not what you can do for your country, for they are liable to tell you.
Mark Steinbeck

Ask not what you can do for your country. Ask what you can do for yourself.
Bob Roberts (1992)

LET OUR OBJECT BE, OUR COUNTRY, OUR WHOLE COUNTRY, AND NOTHING BUT OUR COUNTRY.
DANIEL WEBSTER (1825)

Let us object to our country, our whole country, and nothing but our country.
Hippie Slogan (1960s)

OUR COUNTRY, RIGHT OR WRONG!
STEPHEN DECATUR *SPEECH* (1816)

My country right or wrong is a thing that no patriot would think of saying except in a desperate case. It is like saying my mother, drunk or sober.
G. K. Chesterton *The Defendant*

My country right or left.　　　　　　　　US Newspaper Headline

WHAT THIS COUNTRY NEEDS IS A GOOD FIVE-CENT CIGAR.　　　THOMAS R. MARSHALL *NEW YORK TRIBUNE* (1917)

What this country needs is a good five-cent earthquake.
　　　　　　　　Clifford Odets *Awake and Sing* (1935)

What this country needs is a good five-cent nickel.
　　　　　　　　Franklin P. Adams (1943)

─────────── **" COW "** ───────────

I AM TIED BY THE FOOT UNTIL THE COWS COME HOME.　　　J. ELIOT *ORTHO-EPIA GALLICA* (1593)

I always said that I'd like John Barrymore's acting till the cows came home. Well, ladies and gentlemen, last night the cows came home.
　　　　　　　　George J. Nathan

I could dance with you till the cows come home. Better still, I'll dance with the cows and you can come home.　Groucho Marx *Duck Soup* (1933)

─────────── **" CRIME "** ───────────

CRIME DOESN'T PAY!　　　　　　　ANTI-CRIME SLOGAN

If crime doesn't pay, how come it is one of our biggest businesses?
　　　　　　　　Mitchell Gordon

Crime doesn't pay, sooner or later every criminal gets a parking ticket.
　　　　　　　　Ted Ziegler

Crime doesn't pay; so stop being a criminal and we'll pay you.
　　　　　　　　Eugene Ionesco

Crime doesn't pay . . . like it used to.　　　　American Saying

Poetry is living proof that rhyme doesn't pay.　　　　Anon

─────────── **" CRY "** ───────────

A HUSBAND SHOULD USE HIS WIFE'S SHOULDER TO CRY ON.　　　　　　　IRISH SAYING

There are even times when a dedicated feminist needs a chauvinist to cry on.　　　Clive Cussler *Vixen* (1978)

Every motorway driver, at some time, needs a hard shoulder to pee on.　　　　　　　　Anon

" CULTURE "

WHEN I HEAR THE WORD *CULTURE* I RELEASE THE SAFETY CATCH ON MY REVOLVER.

HANNS JOHST *SCHLAGETER* (1934)

(Commonly attributed to Herman Goering)

When a modern critic hears the word *beauty* he releases the catch on his fountain pen. Dwight MacDonald

When I heard the word *gun*, I reach for my culture.

Dr. I. J. Good *The Scientist Speculates*

On 'The Music Teacher' (1988) – Culture of this kind makes gun-reaching Goerings of us all. Philip French *Observer*

When the British hear the word *culture* they do not, as Goering did, reach for their revolvers; they shuffle nervously from foot to foot, stare at the ceiling and hope that somebody will change the subject.

Francis Whelan *Observer* (1994)

On Sylvia Kelcher (Association of London Authorities) – Whenever 'The Weasel' hears the word *Kelcher*, he will reach for his gun.

'The Weasel' *The Independent* (1994)

" CURSE "

DRINK IS THE CURSE OF THE WORKING CLASSES.

OSCAR WILDE

Work is the curse of the drinking classes. Mike Romanoff

Alimony is the curse of the writing classes. Norman Mailer

Drink is the work of the cursing classes. *The Guardian* (1993)

Graffiti is the curse of the cleaning classes. Graffiti

" DARKEN "

GO, AND NEVER DARKEN MY DOOR, AGAIN.

BENJAMIN FRANKLIN

Go, and never darken my towels again! Groucho Marx *Duck Soup* (1933)

After a French waiter had spilled soup on him – Go, and never darken my Dior again. Noël Coward

❝ DAY ❞

AN APPLE A DAY KEEPS THE DOCTOR AWAY. SAYING

An orgasm a day keeps the doctor away. Mae West

A home run a day will boost my pay. Satchel Paige

A hobby a day keeps the doldrums away.
Phyllis McGinley *A Pocketful of Wry* (1940)

A stanza a day keeps the wolf at bay. Phyllis McGinley *Ibid.*

Two ads a day keeps the sack away. Jeremy Sinclair

An apple a day is 365 a year. American Saying

Six green apples a day makes the doctor stay. American Saying

An apple a day keeps the doctor away and leaves you with a new
esprit de core. Anon

An apple a day keeps the doctor away, unless you get the seeds in
your appendix. Anon

If you ate two apples a day would you keep two doctors away? Anon

Read your bible – a chapter a day keeps Satan away. Anon

An onion a day keeps everyone away. Anon

ANOTHER DAY, ANOTHER DOLLAR. ANON

Another day, another zero. Carl Switzer

Another day, another dolor. Ogden Nash *A Man Can Complain, Can't He?*

A million days, a million dollars.
Anthony Burgess *Times Literary Supplement* (1977)

HE THAT FIGHTS AND RUNS AWAY MAY LIVE TO FIGHT ANOTHER DAY.
NICHOLAS UDALL *ERASMUS' APOPHTHEGMS* (1542)

The man that runs away lives to die another day.
A. E. Housman *The Day of the Battle*

He that loves and runs away may live to love another day. Carolyn Wells

ON A CLEAR DAY YOU CAN SEE FOR EVER.
ALAN JAY LERNER *PLAY TITLE*

On Hollywood producer Irving Thalberg – On a clear day you can see
Thalberg. George S. Kaufman (1930s)

SIX DAYS SHALT THOU LABOUR, AND DO ALL THY WORK, BUT THE SEVENTH DAY IS THE SABBATH OF THE LORD THY GOD.
EXODUS 20:9–10 *THE BIBLE*

Five days shalt thou labour, as the Bible says. The seventh day is the
Lord thy God's. The sixth day is for football. Anthony Burgess

THEY ARE NOT LONG, THE DAYS OF WINE AND ROSES.
ERNEST DOWSON *VITAE SUMMA BREVIS* (1896)

They are not long, the days of whine and neuroses.

Kevin Jackson *The Times* (1990)

WHY, ONE DAY IN THE COUNTRY IS WORTH A MONTH IN TOWN.
CHRISTINA ROSSETTI *SUMMER* (1862)

A day away from Tallulah Bankhead is like a month in the country.

Howard Dietz

———————— ❝ DEAD ❞ ————————

DEAD MEN TELL NO TALES.
JOHN DRYDEN *THE SPANISH FRIAR* (1681)

Dead men tell no tales, but there is many a thing learned in a
wake-house
Irish Saying

Dead men sell no tales.
Carolyn Wells

Dead men rarely tell you anything you want to know. C. F. Adams (1943)

Dead men told no tales, and the living were not always
overcommunicative.
J. Leasor *Love and Land Beyond* (1979)

Dead men tell no solicitors.   Caryl Brahms and S. J. Simon *Don't Tell Mr Disraeli*

HE IS EITHER DEAD OR TEACHING SCHOOL.
ZENOBIUS (100 BC)

He is either dead or my watch has stopped.

Groucho Marx *A Day at the Races* (1937)

———————— ❝ DEATH ❞ ————————

O, DEATH; WHERE IS THY STING?
O, GRAVE, WHERE IS THY VICTORY?
CORINTHIANS 15:55 *THE BIBLE*

O death, where is thy sting-a-ling-ling,
O Grave, thy victoree?
The bells of Hell go ting-a-ling-a-ling
For you but not for me.
BRITISH ARMY SONG (1914)

On Clifford Odets' play 'Clash by Night' – Odets, where is thy sting?

Richard Garland

On 'Evil Dead III' (1993) – O death, where is thy zing?

Jonathan Wilson *The Guardian*

NOTHING CAN BE SAID TO BE CERTAIN EXCEPT DEATH AND TAXES. BENJAMIN FRANKLIN *LETTER* (1789)

That's certain as death and hay-fever. Philip Barry *You and I* (1923)

Death and taxes and childbirth! There's never any convenient time for any of them! Margaret Mitchell *Gone with the Wind* (1936)

TILL DEATH US DO PART. *THE BOOK OF COMMON PRAYER*

Alimony – till debt do us part. Anon

YEA, THOUGH I WALK THROUGH THE VALLEY OF THE SHADOW OF DEATH, I WILL FEAR NO EVIL: FOR THOU ART WITH ME; THY ROD AND STAFF COMFORT ME. PSALMS 23:4 *THE BIBLE*

Though I walk through the Valley of the Shadow of Death, I will fear no evil – 'cos I am the meanest mother-f***er in the whole god-damned country. US Marines Vietnam Slogan

———— ❝ DELIGHTFUL ❞ ————

IT'S DELIGHTFUL, DELICIOUS, DELECTABLE, DELIRIOUS. COLE PORTER *SONG TITLE*

On Desmond Lynam (BBC TV presenter) – He's delightful, he's delicious, he's De-Lynam. Allison Pearson *Independent on Sunday* (1993)

———— ❝ DEVIL ❞ ————

BETWIXT THE DEVIL AND THE DEEP BLUE SEA. ERASMUS *ADAGIA* (1500)

When you're between any sort of devil and the deep blue sea, the deep blue sea sometimes looks very inviting. Terence Rattigan *The Deep Blue Sea* (1952)

The local authorities are caught between the deep blue sea of the rates and the frying pan of the Poll Tax. Anon Conservative MP

———— ❝ DIE ❞ ————

FALSTAFF WILL DIE OF A SWEAT. WILLIAM SHAKESPEARE *HENRY IV, Pt 2* (1591)

False turf will die if it's wet.   Denis Nordern *My Word* (1978)

GOOD AMERICANS, WHEN THEY DIE, GO TO PARIS.

THOMAS GOLD APPLETON (c. 1880)

When good Americans die they go to Paris . . . And when bad Americans die . . . they go to America.

Oscar Wilde *A Woman of No Importance* (1893)

Television? That's where old movies go when they die.

Bob Hope *Academy Award Show* (1952)

On Grantham, Lincolnshire – Centre of the dull world; where the dull go when they die.   Peter Freedman *Glad to be Grey* (1985)

Musical Comedy is where all good jokes go just before they die.   Anon

HE WHOM THE GODS LOVE DIES YOUNG.

MENANDER *DIS EXAPATON* (c. 300 BC)

The best of men cannot suspend their fate:
The good die early, and the bad die late.

Daniel Defoe 'Character of the late Dr S. Annesley'

Only the young die good.   Oliver Herford

I like a man who's good, but not too good. The good die young and I hate a dead one.   Mae West

The good die young – because they see it's no use living if you've got to be good.   John Barrymore

If the good die young, you'll last forever!   Arsenio Hall

Here lies Ezekial Aikle. Aged 102. The good die young.   Anon Epitaph

IF I SHOULD DIE, THINK ONLY THIS OF ME: THAT THERE'S SOME CORNER OF A FOREIGN FIELD THAT IS FOREVER ENGLAND.

RUPERT BROOKE *THE SOLDIER* (1911)

If I should die, think only this of me –
That in some corner of a foreign field
There lies a plagiarist.   Derek Adler

LOVELY AND HONOURABLE IT IS TO DIE FOR ONE'S COUNTRY. (*DULCE ET DECORUM EST PRO PATRIA MORI*)

HORACE *ODES* (19 BC)

The old lie: Dulce et decorum est pro patria mori.

Wilfred Owen *Dulce et decorum est* (1915)

They wrote in the old days that it is sweet and fitting to die for one's country. But in modern war there is nothing sweet nor fitting in your dying. You will die like a dog for no good reason.

Ernest Hemingway

It is a sweet and fitting thing to lie for one's country.   Anon

❝ DISCOVERED ❞

I HAD ALWAYS THOUGHT THAT CLICHÉ WAS A SUBURB OF PARIS, UNTIL I DISCOVERED IT TO BE A STREET IN OXFORD. PHILIP GUEDALLA

I thought that nightingales sang in tune until I discovered Stravinsky.
Graffiti

I used to think squat thrusts were a gym test until I discovered Greek toilets. Graffiti

I thought Muhammad Ali was a street in Cairo until I discovered Smirnoff Vodka. Graffiti

❝ DISTANCE ❞

A STRAIGHT LINE IS THE SHORTEST DISTANCE BETWEEN TWO POINTS. ANON

If there are obstacles, the shortest line between two points may be the crooked one. Bertolt Brecht

A curved line is the loveliest distance between two points. Mae West

Time is the longest distance between two places.
Tennessee Williams *The Glass Menagerie* (1945)

The shortest distance between two jokes makes a perfect speech.
O. A. Battista

A kiss is the shortest distance between two people. Anon

❝ DO ❞

WHEN IN ROME, DO AS THE ROMANS DO.
ST AMBROSE (c. AD 390)

When in Turkey do as the turkeys do. Honoré de Balzac

In Rome, you have to do as the Romans do, or get arrested.
Geoffrey Harmsworth (1935)

When you're in Korea, you have to eat as the Romans do. Tony Francis

❝ DOG ❞

A BARKING DOG NEVER BITES. FRENCH PROVERB (1250)

A bargain dog never bites. Ogden Nash *Funereal Reflection* (1940)

Barking dogs never bite – but they don't know that. Sholem Aleichem

DOG BITES MAN IS NOT NEWS, BUT MAN BITES DOG, THAT IS NEWS. JOHN B. BOGART *NEW YORK SUN* (1880)

If a man bites a dog, that used to be news. It isn't any more. It has to be: *Father of Ten Bites Titled Woman's Chow.* Tod Claymore (1939)

She poisoned his hot dog. Man bites dog and – zowie. Ellery Queen *Man Bites Dog* (1940)

DOG EAT DOG. LATIN PROVERB

Dog won't eat dog, but men will eat each other up like cannibals. C. H. Spurgeon (1869)

Boxing is a business. It's a case of dog eat dog, and I'm not about to be eaten. Brian Baronet

Show business is dog eat dog. It's worse than dog eat dog. It's dog doesn't return other dog's phone calls. Woody Allen *Crimes and Misdemeanours* (1989)

It's dog eat dog in this rat race. John Deacon

It's a dog-eat-dog world and I'm wearing Milk Bones underwear. George Wendt *Cheers* – NBC TV (1992)

That's nature . . . it's the dog-eat-dog world that these fish live in. John Wilson

Someone once said it's a dog eat dog world, I think it was a chihuahua. DHL Advert

You know how it is in the kid's book world: It's just bunny eat bunny. Anon publisher

EVERY DOG HAS ITS DAY. RICHARD TAVERNER *ERASMUS' ADAGES* (1545)

Every dogma must have its day. Carolyn Wells

Every dog has its day, and every cat its night. H. W. Thompson (1940)

Every dog deserves his day. M. Craig *Were He a Stranger* (1978)

Every dog must have his day, and every bitch two Sunday afternoons. Naval Saying

Every dog must have his day . . . and his bone, his walk . . . Anon

GIVE A DOG A BAD NAME, AND HANG HIM. JOHN STEVENS *DICTIONARY* (1706)

Give a dog a bad name, and if you give a man or a race of men an ill name, they are very likely to do something that deserves hanging. Sir Walter Scott *Guy Mannering* (1815)

Give a dog a bad name, they say; call a woman a mother-in-law, and
    it's the same thing. Margaret Oliphant *Second Son* (1888)

LET SLEEPING DOGS LIE.

GEOFFREY CHAUCER *TROILUS AND CRESSIDA* (1385)

Let sleeping dogs lie, but why let lying dogs sleep? Herbert Beerbohm

Let sleeping dogs lie until you gets bitten by them. G.H. and M. Cole (1942)

Very much better to let sleeping years lie. F. B. Young (1942)

Remember, everybody, let sleeping dogs lie, but somebody wake up
    the president. Bill Cosby

—————— ❝ DOING ❞ ——————

WHATEVER IS WORTH DOING AT ALL IS WORTH
DOING WELL. LORD PHILIP CHESTERFIELD *LETTER* (1746)

The prime truth of woman, the universal mother: that if a thing is
    worth doing, it is worth doing badly.
G. K. Chesterton *What's Wrong with the World* (1910)

What is worth doing is worth the trouble of asking somebody to do it.
Ambrose Bierce *The Devil's Dictionary* (1911)

If you want work well done, select a busy man; the other kind has no
    time. Elbert Hubbard *The Note Book* (1927)

If a thing's worth doing, it's worth doing late. Frederick Oliver

What's worth doing is worth doing for money. Joseph Donohoe

Anything that is worth doing has been done frequently. Things
    hitherto undone should be given, I suspect, a wide berth.
Max Beerbohm

When a thing is not worth overdoing, leave it alone. Henry H. Haskins

If a thing isn't worth doing, it isn't worth doing well. Sydney J. Harris

Whatever is worth doing at all, is worth doing tomorrow. Anon

—————— ❝ DONKEY ❞ ——————

SHE COULD TALK THE HIND LEG OFF A DONKEY.

ANON SAYING

He could eat the hind leg off a donkey. Anon

❝ DOUBT ❞

WHEN IN DOUBT FOLLOW THE SUIT OF THE WISE AND THE PRUDENT; SOONER OR LATER THEY WILL WIN THE ODD TRICK.

BALTASAAR GRACIAN *THE MANUAL ORACLE* (1647)

As to the adjective; when in doubt, strike it out. Mark Twain

When in doubt, mumble; when in trouble, delegate; when in charge, ponder. James H. Boren

When in doubt, shout! S. Major Jones (1961)

When in doubt make a fool of yourself. There is a microscopically thin line between being brilliant and creative and acting like the most gigantic idiot on earth. So what the hell, leap.

Cynthia Heimel *Village Voice* (1983)

When in doubt, jump. Malcolm Forbes

When in doubt, ascribe all quotations to Bernard Shaw. Nigel Rees

When in doubt, file under *H* for Haven't A Clue. Roger Kilroy

When in doubt, don't. Saul W. Gellerman *Harvard Business Review* (1988)

When in doubt, fry the nearest bad guy.

Damon Wayans *The Last Boy Scout* (1991)

When in doubt, shut up. Anon

When in debt, use credit cards. Anon

❝ DO UNTO . . . ❞

WHAT YOU DO NOT WANT DONE TO YOURSELF, DO NOT DO TO OTHERS. CONFUCIUS *ANALECTS* (500 BC)

Do unto the other feller the way he'd like to do unto you, an' do it first. Edward N. Westcott *David Harum* (1898)

Do not do unto others as you would they should do unto you. Their tastes may not be the same.

George Bernard Shaw *Maxims for Revolutionists* (1903)

Do unto yourself as your neighbours do unto themselves and look pleasant. George Ade *Hand-made Fables* (1920)

Do to others that which you do not wish them to do to you.

James Huneker (1920)

Do unto others as you would have others do unto you. But better not expect others to do unto you what you do unto them. Chen Chiju

Don't do for others what you wouldn't think of asking them to do for you. Josh Billings

Do unto others, but be careful – someone may squeal.

Bill Cosby *You Bet Your Life* (1993)

Do unto others before they do you. Anon

Do knot undo others. Anon

—————— **"DREAMS"** ——————

... WE ARE SUCH STUFF
AS DREAMS ARE MADE ON.

WILLIAM SHAKESPEARE *THE TEMPEST* (1612)

Religions are such stuff as dreams are made of.

H. G. Wells *The Happy Turning* (1946)

Winston Churchill on top of a wave has in him the stuff that tyrants are made of. Lord Beaverbrook

It is of such stuff and nonsense that dreams are made on. Clifton Fadiman

We have such staff as dreams are made of. Anon personnel agency slogan

—————— **"DRESSED"** ——————

WHEN YOU'RE ALL DRESSED UP AND NO PLACE TO
GO.

G. WHITING *SONG TITLE* (1912)

All dressed up and don't know Huerto Go. Cole Porter (1914)

A dead atheist is someone who's all dressed up with no place to go.

James Duffecy *New York Times* (1964)

—————— **"DRINK"** ——————

DON'T DRINK AND DRIVE. GOVERNMENT DRIVING CAMPAIGN

If you drink, don't drive – don't even putt. Dean Martin

I never drink when I drive, only when my wife does. Car bumper sticker

—————— **"DRUM"** ——————

NOT A DRUM WAS HEARD, NOT A FUNERAL NOTE,
AS HIS CORSE TO THE RAMPART WE HURRIED.

CHARLES WOLFE *THE BURIAL OF SIR JOHN MOORE* (1817)

Not a drum was heard, not a funeral note,
As his horse on the ramparts we curried. Anon

"DRY"

HARDLY A DRY EYE IN THE HOUSE. ANON

Hardly a dry glass in the house. Campbell Burnap *Jazz FM* (1993)

"DUCK"

I ALWAYS TOOK TO SHOOTING LIKE A DUCK TO WATER. SIR J. ASTLEY *FIFTY YEARS OF MY LIFE* (1894)

On Erin Pizzey (Author) – She took to writing romances like a duck
to orange sauce. Julie Burchill *Born-again Cows* (1984)

And he took to it like water to a duck. Richard Pitman

He's taken to the good life like champagne off a duck's back.
Kathy Lette (1993)

He took to it like a duck to a down pillow. Anon

"DUTY"

ENGLAND EXPECTS EVERY MAN WILL DO HIS DUTY.
LORD NELSON *REMARK AT THE BATTLE OF TRAFALGAR* (1805)

During the First World War – England expects every American to do
his duty. American Saying (1917)

On Theodore Roosevelt's visit to Africa – Wall Street expects every lion
to do its duty. Anon Wall Street Sign

India expects every man to do his dhoti. Sir Edwyn Lutyens (1920)

Banner at the Liverpool v Everton FA Cup Final – Liverpool expects
Everton to do its duty. Anon (1986)

"EAGLE"

THE EAGLE HAS LANDED. APOLLO XI SPACE MISSION (1969)

The Beagle has landed. Charles M. Schultz *Peanuts*

On ski-jumper Eddie 'The Eagle' Edwards – The Eagle has crash
landed. *The Sun*

"EAR"

HE THAT HATH EARS TO HEAR, LET HIM HEAR.

MATTHEW *THE BIBLE*

He that hath ears to listen let him stuff them with cotton.

William M. Thackeray

IN ONE EAR AND OUT THE OTHER.   QUINTILIAN (c. AD 100)

He comes in at one year. To go out by the other!

Thomas Hood *Ode to the Late Lord Mayor* (1825)

Gossip goes in one ear and over the back fence.   Anon

WALLS HAVE EARS.   *TALMUD* (450)

Walls have ears – I've just found one in one of their pork pies.   Graffiti

WHERE MORE IS MEANT THAN MEETS THE EAR.

JOHN MILTON *IL PENSEROSO* (1632)

On 'Algavine and Selysette' – There is less in this than meets the eye.

Talullah Bankhead

There's a lot of juice in this grapefruit, more than meets the eye.   Anon

"EAST"

OH, EAST IS EAST, AND WEST IS WEST, AND NEVER THE TWAIN SHALL MEET.

RUDYARD KIPLING *THE BALLAD OF EAST AND WEST*

East is East, and West is San Francisco, according to Californians.

O. Henry (1910)

"EAT"

LET US EAT AND DRINK; FOR TOMORROW WE SHALL DIE.   ISAIAH 22:13 *THE BIBLE*

Eat, drink, and be leary.   O. Henry (1908)

Drink and dance and laugh and lie,
Love, the reeling midnight through,
For tomorrow we shall die!
(But, alas, we never do.)   Dorothy Parker *The Flaw in Plagiarism* (1936)

Eat, drink, and be merry, for tomorrow and tomorrow and tomorrow
    roll on their dreary course.   E. S. Gardner (1943)

On food allergies – Eat, drink and be wary.   *Sunday Telegraph* (1994)

Eat, drink and be merry, for tomorrow we shall diet.   Anon

Eat, drink and drink, for tomorrow we shall be dry.   Anon

Eat, drink and be merry, for tomorrow we may not die after all. Graffiti

TELL ME WHAT YOU EAT AND I WILL TELL YOU WHAT YOU ARE.

ANTHELME BRILLAT-SAVARIN *PHYSIOLOGIE DU GOUT* (1825)

You are not what you eat; but where you eat is who you are.

Paul Theroux

You are what you throw away.   A. J. Weberman (1971)

You are what you beat.   Boxing maxim

Scientists say we are what we eat. Nuts must be a commoner diet than
we had thought.   Anon

If you are what you eat, a visit to North Carolina could make you a
very interesting person.   Anon

You are what you wear.   Anon

——————— ❝ EGGS ❞ ———————

DON'T PUT ALL YOUR EGGS IN ONE BASKET.

MIGUEL DE CERVANTES *DON QUIXOTE* (1615)

PUT all your eggs in one basket and watch that basket. Mark Twain (1893)

On having an abortion – That teaches me to put all my eggs in one
bastard.   Dorothy Parker

On a fatal stampede after a fire in a theatre in northern Spain – Don't
put all your Basques in one exit.   Franklin P. Adams

WE CANNOT MAKE OMELETTES WITHOUT BREAKING EGGS.   FRENCH PROVERB

Hollywood can't make a Hamlet without breaking a few egos.

William Goldman (1984)

You can't make an omelette without frying eggs.   Bill Deedes

Thatcherites are people who say you can't make omelettes without
breaking eggs, but imagine that the mere breaking of the eggs will
produce omelettes.   Julian Critchley *Some of Us* (1992)

❝ ELECTRA ❞

MOURNING BECOMES ELECTRA.
EUGENE O'NEILL *PLAY TITLE* (1931)

Electra becomes morbid.
Ogden Nash *Book title* (1933)

❝ ENCOUNTERS ❞

CLOSE ENCOUNTERS OF THE THIRD KIND.
J. ALLEN HYNEK *THING FROM ANOTHER WORLD* (1951)

Close Encounters of the Furred Kind
Evening Standard

Clothes Encounters.
The Guardian

Close In Contours.
The Guardian

Unclothed Encounters of the Bird Kind.
Mayfair

Illegal Aliens of the Third Kind.
Omni

Close Encounters with the Third Reich.
Vogue

Close Encounters of the Thud Kind.
Graffiti on a hoarding advertising a meteor show at the Planetarium, in Wellington, New Zealand.

Roman Polanski's latest movie – Close Encounters with the Third
Grade.
American Graffiti

❝ END ❞

ALL'S WELL THAT ENDS WELL.
EURIPIDES (410 BC)

All's swell that ends swell.
H. S. Keeler (1941)

All's well that ends with a good meal.
Arnold Lobel (1980)

On Orson Welles (Actor/Director) – All's well that ends Welles.
Jack Fier (*See Welles' reply under Fear*)

THE END JUSTIFIES THE MEANS.
OVID (10 BC)

The ends justify the genes.
Graffiti

IF ALL THE ECONOMISTS WERE LAID END TO END, THEY WOULD NOT REACH A CONCLUSION.
G. B. SHAW

On the ladies at the Yale Prom – If all these young ladies were laid end
to end, I wouldn't be surprised.
Dorothy Parker

Walt Whitman, who laid end to end words never seen in each other's
company before, outside of a dictionary.
David Lodge

If you laid all our laws end to end, there would be no end.

Arthur 'Bugs' Baer

If all the nation's economists were laid end to end, they would still point in all directions.

Arthur H. Motley

If all Britain's heavyweight boxers were laid end to end, we wouldn't be surprised.

Ring magazine

If all the college boys who slept in class were placed end to end, they would be much more comfortable.

Anon

If all the automobiles in the world were laid end to end, it would be a Sunday afternoon.

Anon

If all the road-hogs were laid end to end, that would be Utopia.   Anon

If you laid the Chinese end to end around the world, do you know that you'd drown half of them?

Graffiti

On the dramatic form of tragedy – **NOW A WHOLE IS THAT WHICH HAS A BEGINNING, A MIDDLE AND AN END.**

ARISTOTLE *POETICS* (c. 350 BC)

Every book should have a beginning, a muddle and an end.

Peter de Vries

I like a film to have a beginning, a middle, and an end, but not necessarily in that order.

Jean-Luc Godard

BURN THE CANDLE AT BOTH ENDS.

RANDLE COTGRAVE *FRENCH AND ENGLISH TONGUE* (1611)

They are burning both ends of the scandal.

Phyllis McGinley *Why, Some of my Best Friends are Women* (1940)

On a jaded darts player – He's been burning the midnight oil at both ends.

Sid Waddell

People always say I shouldn't be burning the candle at both ends. Maybe because they don't have a big enough candle.   George Best

If you burn the candle at both ends, you may be able to make both ends meet.

Anon

If you burn the candle at both ends, you are not so bright as you think.

Anon

—————— **" ENGLAND "** ——————

OH, TO BE IN ENGLAND, NOW THAT APRIL'S THERE.

ROBERT BROWNING *HOME THOUGHTS FROM ABROAD* (1840)

On Lady June Inverclyde appearing on the New York stage – Oh, to be in England, now that June's here.   Robert Garland

Oh, to be in LA when the polyethyl-vinyl trees are in bloom.   Herb Gold

**THERE'LL ALWAYS BE AN ENGLAND
WHILE THERE'S A COUNTRY LANE.**
                              CLARKE ROSS PARKER *THERE'LL ALWAYS BE AN ENGLAND*

There'll always be an England – even if it's in Hollywood.   Bob Hope

—————— ❝ EQUAL ❞ ——————

**ALL MEN ARE CREATED EQUAL, AND ARE
DISTINGUISHED ALONE BY VIRTUE.**   LATIN PROVERB

All men are created equal, but quite a few eventually get over it.
                                                          Lord Mancroft

All men are equal – except myself.   Sir Herbert Beerbohm Tree (1906)

All men are equal – all men, that is to say, who possess umbrellas.
                                              E. M. Forster *Howard's End* (1910)

All animals are created equal, but some animals are more equal than
others.   George Orwell *Animal Farm* (1945)

To some lawyers, all facts are created equal.   Felix Frankfurter

All men are equal on the turf and under it.   Lord George Bentinck

All men are cremated equal.   Goodman Ace

If men are created equal, who do you trust?   Joan Collins

All are created equal, it's just some work harder in the off-season.
                              Reebok American football boot advert (1993)

All men are created equal, but it's what we are equal to that's important.   Anon

—————— ❝ EVIL ❞ ——————

**THE EVIL THAT MEN DO LIVES AFTER THEM,
THE GOOD IS OFT INTERRED WITH THEIR BONES.**
                              WILLIAM SHAKESPEARE *JULIUS CAESAR* (1599)

The evil that men do lives after them. Yes, and a good deal of the evil
that they never did as well.   Samuel Butler *Note Books* (1912)

HEAR NO EVIL, SEE NO EVIL, SPEAK NO EVIL.
                                                    CHINESE PROVERB

General Eisenhower employs the three-monkeys standard of campaign morality: see no evil – if it's Republican; hear no evil – unless it's Democratic; and speak no evil – unless Senator Taft says it's all right.
Adlai Stevenson

On US Presidents Carter, Ford and Nixon – See No Evil, Hear No Evil and Evil.
Robert J. Dole (1983)

Hear no evil, see no evil, think no evil, and you'll never write a best-selling novel.
Dan Bennett

Hear no evil, see no evil, speak no evil, and you'll never be a success at a cocktail party.
Anon

IT IS BETTER TO CHOOSE THE LESSER OF TWO EVILS.
ARISTOPHANES (393 BC)

A pessimist is one who, when he has the choice of two evils, chooses both.
Oscar Wilde

Of two evils, choose the prettier.
Carolyn Wells

When choosing between two evils I always like to take the one I've never tried before.
Mae West *Klondike Annie* (1936)

Of two evils, choose neither.
Charles Spurgeon

Of two evils, when we tell ourselves we are choosing the lesser, we usually mean we are choosing the more comfortable.
Sydney Harris

On Lynn, wife of Frank Loesser – She is the evil of two Loessers.
Harry Kurnitz

When you choose the lesser of two evils, always remember that it is still an evil.
Max Lerner *The Unfinished Country* (1959)

In the past naval cooking at sea involved a choice between the lesser of two weevils.
Anon

―――――――― " EXIST " ――――――――

IF GOD DID NOT EXIST, IT WOULD BE NECESSARY TO INVENT HIM.
VOLTAIRE *EPITRES*

On entertainer Oscar Levant – A character who, had he not existed, could not be imagined.
S. N. Behrman

If the cinema did not exist, only Nicholas Ray would be capable of inventing it.
Jean-Luc Godard

If snooker hadn't existed, TV would surely have had to invent it.
Geoffrey Nicholson

On author Quentin Crisp – If he had never existed, it is unlikely that anyone would have had the nerve to invent him.
The Times

If death did not exist, the cinema would have had to invent it.
David Thomson *Independent on Sunday* (1994)

❝ EXPANDS ❞

WORK EXPANDS TO FILL THE TIME AVAILABLE FOR ITS COMPLETION. C. NORTHCOTE PARKINSON *THE LISTENER* (1955)

The volume of paper expands to fill the available briefcases.
Jerry Brown (1973)

News expands to fill the time and space allotted to its coverage.
William Safire *New York Times* (1973)

Optimism expands to fill the scope available for its exercise. *Merrow's Law*

Runs expand to fill the number of overs available.
M.J.K. Smith's Law of Limited Overs Cricket

Housework expands to fill the time available plus half an hour.
Shirley Conran *Superwoman 2*

❝ EYES ❞

EYE FOR EYE, TOOTH FOR TOOTH . . .
EXODUS 21:23 *THE BIBLE*

When two egotists meet, it's a case of an I for an I. Anon

An eye for an eye, and very soon the whole world will be blind. Graffiti

IF THINE EYE OFFEND THEE, PLUCK IT OUT, AND CAST IT FROM THEE. MATTHEW *THE BIBLE*

On Aneurin 'Nye' Bevan (Labour politician) – If thy Nye offend thee,
pluck it out. Clement Attlee

At the Battle of Bunker Hill (1775) – **MEN, YOU ARE ALL MARKSMEN, DON'T ONE OF YOU FIRE UNTIL YOU SEE THE WHITES OF THEIR EYES.**
GENERAL ISRAEL PUTNAM (1775)

To the 405th Squadron fighting the Japanese in World War II – Don't
fire until you see the slant of their eyes. Lieutenant Mortimer Smith (1943)

MINE EYES HAVE SEEN THE GLORY OF THE COMING OF THE LORD.
JULIA WARD HOWE *BATTLE HYMN OF THE REPUBLIC* (1861)

Mayonnaise . . . have seen the glory of the coming of the Lord!
Knock-knock joke

A SIGHT FOR SORE EYES. JONATHAN SWIFT

A traffic jam is a site for sore guys. Anon

" FACE "

I REMEMBER YOUR FACE PERFECTLY, BUT I JUST CAN'T THINK OF YOUR NAME.   ANON

I remember your name perfectly, but I just can't think of your face.
Dr. W. A. Spooner

I never forget a face, but in your case I'll make an exception.
Groucho Marx

I don't recall your name, but the manners are familiar.   Oliver Herford

NICE LEGS, SHAME ABOUT THE FACE.

THE MONKS *SONG TITLE* (1979)

Nice video, shame about the song.   *Not the Nine O'Clock News* – BBC TV
Nice face, shame about the breath.   Listerine Mouthwash Advert

WAS THIS THE FACE THAT LAUNCH'D A THOUSAND SHIPS . . . ?   CHRISTOPHER MARLOWE *DOCTOR FAUSTUS* (1604)

This is the face that burnt a thousand boats.
G. B. Shaw *The Admirable Bashville* (1926)

On Florence Horsbrugh (Minister for Education) – This is the face
which has sunk a thousand scholarships.   Aneurin Bevan *Speech* (1953)

On Glenda Jackson (Actress) – She has a face to launch a thousand
dredgers.   Jack De Manio

On Debbie Harry (Singer) – The face that launched a thousand
whores.   'The Stud Brothers' *Melody Maker*

On Tuesday Weld (Actress) – The face that almost launched a
thousand scripts.   Allen Berra (1989)

" FAIR "

ALL'S FAIR IN LOVE AND WAR, YOU KNOW.

NATHAN FORREST

All is fair in love, war and parliamentary procedure.   Michael Foot
All is fair in love and golf.   American saying

❝ FAITH ❞

FAITH CAN MOVE MOUNTAINS. MATTHEW *THE BIBLE*

Faith can certainly remove a mountain of evidence. Samuel Butler

Faith can move mountains but not furniture. Anon

Faith either moves mountains or tunnels underneath. Anon

Doubt makes the mountain which faith can move. Anon

❝ FAMILIARITY ❞

FAMILIARITY BREEDS CONTEMPT. AESOP *FABLES* (570 BC)

Though familiarity may not breed contempt, it takes the edge off
admiration. William Hazlitt (1821)

Familiarity breeds contempt – and children. Mark Twain

I like familiarity. In me it does not breed contempt. Only more
familiarity. Gertrude Stein

Familiarity breeds attempt. Goodman Ace

Familiarity breeds contentment. George Ade *Hand-Made Fables* (1920)

Familiarity breeds. L. L. Levinson

Familiarity breeds over-population. L. L. Levinson

Family tea breeds contempt. Graffiti

❝ FAMILIES ❞

**ACCIDENTS WILL HAPPEN IN THE BEST REGULATED
FAMILIES.** P. ATALL *HERMIT IN AMERICA* (1819)

Actresses will happen in the best regulated families. Oliver Herford

Cuckoos will happen in the nest regulated families. Anon

❝ FAMILY ❞

**THE FAMILY THAT PRAYS TOGETHER STAYS
TOGETHER.** AL SCALPONE

The family that plays together, stays together. *Parents' Magazine* (1954)

The family that spies together, sties together. R. Hill *Spy's Wife* (1980)

Couples who cook together stay together (Maybe because they can't
decide who'll get the Cuisinart). Erica Jong

On 'Addams Family Values' (1993) – For the family that preys
 together.
                                                          Philip French *Observer*

The family that shoots together, loots together.
                                                                          Graffiti

The family that flays together, stays together.
                                                                          Graffiti

❝ FAT ❞

I'M FAT, BUT THIN INSIDE. HAS IT EVER STRUCK
YOU THAT THERE'S A THIN MAN INSIDE EVERY FAT
MAN, JUST AS THEY SAY THERE IS A STATUE INSIDE
EVERY BLOCK OF STONE.
                         GEORGE ORWELL *COMING UP FOR AIR* (1939)

Imprisoned in every fat man is a thin one wildly signalling to be let
 out.
                              Cyril Connolly *The Unquiet Grave* (1944)

Enclosing every thin man, there's a fat man demanding elbow-room.
                         Evelyn Waugh *Officers and Gentlemen* (1954)

Outside every fat man is an even fatter man trying to close in.
                         Kingsley Amis *One Fat Englishman* (1963)

It seems to me that outside every thin girl is a fat man, trying to get
 in.
                                            Katharine Whitehorn

Inside every fat Englishman is a thin Hindu trying to get out.
                                                        Timothy Leary

On Geoff Capes (Shot-putter) – Somewhere inside that flabby body
 was an athlete trying to get out.
                                                          Stuart Storey

❝ FATHER ❞

FULL FATHOM FIVE THY FATHER LIES;
OF HIS BONES ARE CORAL MADE:
THOSE ARE PEARLS THAT WERE HIS EYES:
NOTHING OF HIM DOTH FADE.
                    WILLIAM SHAKESPEARE *THE TEMPEST* (1611)

Full fathom five thy father lies,
His aqualung was the wrong size.
                                                    June M. Langfield

" FAVOUR "

ALL THOSE IN FAVOUR . . . PLEASE RAISE YOUR RIGHT HAND.
ANON SAYING

All those in favour of conserving gasoline please raise your right foot.
California highway sign

" FEAR "

LET ME ASSERT MY FIRM BELIEF THAT THE ONLY THING WE HAVE TO FEAR IS FEAR ITSELF.
FRANKLIN D. ROOSEVELT (1933)

On Jack Fier (Film Production Manager) – We have nothing to fear, but Fier himself.
Orson Welles

We have nothing to fear but sanity itself.
Robin Williams

" FEED "

FEED A COLD AND STARVE A FEVER.
ENGLISH PROVERB

One nanny said, *Feed a cold*; she was a neo-Keynesian. Another nanny said, *Starve a cold*; she was a monetarist.
Harold MacMillan (1984)

" FEET "

A MAN WITH BOTH FEET FIRMLY PLANTED ON THE GROUND.
ANON SAYING

A radical is a man with both feet firmly planted in the air.
Franklin D. Roosevelt *Fireside Chat* (1939)

An egghead is one who stands firmly on both feet in mid-air on both sides of an issue.
Homer Ferguson (1954)

A conservative is a man with both feet firmly planted in his mouth.
Anon

A hippie is one with both feet firmly planted in their sandals.
Anon

❝ FEMALE ❞

THE FEMALE OF THE SPECIES IS MORE DEADLY THAN THE MALE. RUDYARD KIPLING *MORNING POST* (1911)

The female of the species is more practical than the male.
Patricia Wentworth *In the Balance* (1941)

The female of the species is more dead pan than the male.
Jean Webb *No Match for Murder* (1942)

We know phrases about the female of the species being more deadly than the male, but the suffragettes seemed to have gone into abeyance. *The Guardian* (1979)

On after-dinner speaking – The female of the speeches is more deadly than the meal. Frank Muir *My Word* (1980)

The female of the speechless . . . John Naughton *Observer* (1993)

❝ FIRE ❞

C'MON BABY LIGHT MY FIRE.
JIM MORRISON *LIGHT MY FIRE* (1967)

C'mon Colmans, light my fire. Mustard Advert (1979)

HE WORKS AND BLOWS THE COALS AND HAS PLENTY OF OTHER IRONS IN THE FIRE.
ARISTOPHANES (c. 400 BC)

On Gore Vidal's 'Two Sisters' – There are too many ironies in the fire.
John Leonard *New York Times* (1970)

❝ FLAG ❞

STOOD FOR HIS COUNTRY GLORY FAST AND NAILED HER FLAG TO THE MAST. Sir Walter Scott *Marmion* (1808)

The trouble with Winston Churchill is that he nails his trousers to the mast and can't climb down. Clement Attlee

The Home Secretary has nailed his flag to the wall. Don Concannon

So you've finally nailed your mast to Neil Kinnock? Anon

THE PEOPLE'S FLAG IS DEEPEST RED;
IT SHROUDED OFT OUR MARTYRED DEAD,
AND ERE THEIR LIMBS GREW STIFF AND COLD,
THEIR HEART'S BLOOD DYED ITS EVERY FOLD.
THEN RAISE THE SCARLET STANDARD HIGH!
WITHIN ITS SHADE WE'LL LIVE OR DIE.
THO' COWARDS FLINCH AND TRAITORS SNEER,
WE'LL KEEP THE RED FLAG FLYING HERE.

JAMES M. CONNELL *THE RED FLAG* (1889)

The Tories' flag is deepest blue,
Blue blood has stained it through and through.
But Tories now aren't chinless fools,
They're sharp young men from grammar schools.
So let us have a new flag that's
Appropriate for technocrats.
Let's sing and dance down Brighton Pier
And fly the skull and crossbones here.   Chris Miller

❝ FOLD ❞

THE CARES THAT INFEST THE DAY
SHALL FOLD THEIR TENTS LIKE THE ARABS,
AND SILENTLY STEAL AWAY.

HENRY WADSWORTH LONGFELLOW *THE DAY IS DONE*

On his poker winnings – I fold my tens like the Arabs, and silently
    steal away.   George S. Kaufman

❝ FOOL ❞

A FISHING ROD HAS A FOOL AT ONE END AND A
WORM AT THE OTHER.   SAMUEL JOHNSON

A cigarette has a fool at one end and a fire at the other.   Anon (1918)

A FOOL AND HIS MONEY ARE SOON PARTED

J. BRIDGES *DEFENCE OF GOVERNMENT* (1616)

A fool and his words are soon parted; a man of genius and his money.
William Shenstone *Essays on Man and Manners*

A rich man and his daughter are soon parted.   Kin Hubbard

A middle aged American and his money are soon parted – if you
    make him believe he is sick.   Maximillian Muller *Alkaloid Clinic* (1904)

A fool and his money are soon married. Carolyn Wells

A fool and his money are soon invited out. *Merit Puzzle Plus*

A fool and his money were lucky to get together in the first place.
Gambler's Saying

A fool and his money sooner or later wind up in college. Anon

A fool and his money may soon be parted, but not a fool and his car.
Anon

A fool and his money are soon partying. Anon

A widow and her money are soon courted. Anon

FOR FOOLS RUSH IN WHERE ANGELS FEAR TO TREAD. ALEXANDER POPE *ESSAY ON CRITICISM* (1711)

A kind of mixture of fools and angels – they rush in and fear to tread
at the same time. O. Henry *The Moment of Victory*

You were treading where no man fears to go. Ron Pickering

Fools drive around on tyres no mechanic would fear to tread. Anon

SUFFER FOOLS GLADLY. 2 CORINTHIANS *THE BIBLE*

The Irish people do not gladly suffer common sense.
Oliver St John Gogarty (1935)

Suffer fools gladly. They may be right.
Holbrook Jackson *Platitudes in the Making*

On comedian Kenneth Williams – He suffers fools by gladly making
them suffer. Sheila Hancock

THERE'S NO FOOL LIKE AN OLD FOOL. PROVERB

In the garage, there's no fool like an oiled fool. Anon

There's no fool like an old fool – just ask a young fool. Anon

YOU CAN FOOL ALL THE PEOPLE SOME OF THE TIME, AND SOME OF THE PEOPLE ALL THE TIME, BUT YOU CANNOT FOOL ALL THE PEOPLE ALL THE TIME. ABRAHAM LINCOLN *SPEECH* (1856)

You *can* fool most of the people most of the time. P. T. Barnum

You can fool all the people all the time if the advertising is right and
the budget is big enough. Joseph E. Levine

You can fool too many of the people too much of the time.
James Thurber *The Owl Who Was Good*

You can fool some of the people all of the time and all of the people
some of the time – except when you're in a swimming costume.
Gene Perret

You can't fool all of the people all of the time but most of us try. Anon

You can't fool all of the people all of the time, but it isn't necessary.
A majority will do. Anon

You can fool some of the people all of the time and all of the people
some of the time and the rest of the time somebody else will fool
them. Anon

—— " FOOT " ——

HE'S AN OLD TWADDLER WITH ONE FOOT ALREADY IN THE GRAVE. PLUTARCH *MORALIA* (AD 100)

That old man with one foot in the grave . . . and the other three in
the cash box. Thornton Wilder *The Matchmaker*

I've got one foot in the grate . . . I want to be cremated. Max Kauffman

Pretoria has one foot in the nineteenth century and the other in
Woolworths. Christopher Hope *White Boy Running*

One foot in the groove. Craig Brown *Sunday Times* (1993)

YOU SHOULD . . . PUT YOUR BEST FOOT FORWARD!
WILLIAM CONGREVE *THE WAY OF THE WORLD* (1693)

It's ungrammatical to talk about putting your best foot forward unless
you're a quadruped. Lambert Jeffries

It must be difficult for two-faced people to put their best face forward. Anon

—— " FORGIVE " ——

ONE CAN FORGIVE ANYTHING EXCEPT GOOD DAYS.
DUTCH PROVERB

After a good dinner, one can forgive anybody, even one's own
relatives. Oscar Wilde

Men will forgive anything except bad prose. Sir Winston Churchill

ONE SHOULD FORGIVE ONE'S ENEMIES, BUT NOT BEFORE THEY ARE HANGED. HEINRICH HEINE (c. 1850)

You should forgive your enemies, but never forget their names. Robert F. Kennedy

FOUR

Four good mothers beget four bad daughters: Great familiarity –
contempt, Truth – hatred, Virtue – envy, Riches – ignorance.

Countryman (1647)

There are four stages of marriage: First, there's the affair, then the
marriage, then children and finally the fourth stage, without which
you cannot know a woman, divorce. Norman Mailer (1969)

Four things I'd been better without: Love, curiosity, freckles and
doubt. Dorothy Parker *Inventory*

I've got four things to live by: don't say nothin' that will hurt anybody; don't give advice, nobody will take it anyway; don't
complain; don't explain. Edward Scott *Last words* (1954)

The world may be divided into people that read, people that write,
people that think, and fox-hunters.

William Shenstone *On Writing and Books* (1764)

There are four types of men in the world: lovers, opportunists,
lookers-on, and imbeciles. The happiest are the imbeciles.

Hippolyte Taine *Life and Opinions of Thomas Graingorge* (1867)

Four things not to trust: a dog's tooth, a horse's hoof, a cow's horn,
and an Englishman's laugh. T. H. White *Elephant and Kangaroo* (1948)

The four most important words in the English language are I, me,
mine and money. Anon

━━ **"FREE"** ━━

THERE IS NO SUCH THING AS A FREE LUNCH.

MILTON FRIEDMAN Attrib.

On the high cost of space travel – There is no such thing as a free
launch. Richard Gephardt

There is no such thing as a free lunch, but there is a cheap one.

New York Times (1979)

There is no such thing as a calorie-free lunch. Colin M. Jarman

━━ **"FREEZE"** ━━

IT'S COLD ENOUGH TO FREEZE THE BALLS OFF A
BRASS MONKEY.

ANON SAYING

It's cold enough to freeze the brass buttons off a flunkey
The Two Ronnies – BBC TV (1973)

It's cold enough to freeze a jolly good fellow.   Adrian Love *Jazz FM* (1992)

❝ FRENCH ❞

THERE HAS ALWAYS BEEN SOMETHING FISHY ABOUT THE FRENCH.   NOEL COWARD *CONVERSATION PIECE*

There has always been something Vichy about the French.
Ivor Novello *Ambrosia and Small Beer*

❝ FRIEND ❞

DIAMONDS ARE A GIRL'S BEST FRIEND.
LEO ROBIN *SONG TITLE* (1949)

Rough diamonds are a girl's best friend.   Jilly Cooper

How come when diamonds are a girl's best friend, man's best friend is his dog?   Anon

A bra is a girl's best friend.   Anon advert (c. 1950)

A FRIEND IN NEED IS A FRIEND INDEED.
PLAUTUS (c. 200 BC)

A friend in need is a friend to be avoided.   Herbert Samuel

A friend in power is a friend lost.   Henry B. Adams

A friend that isn't in need is a friend indeed.   Kin Hubbard

A friend in need is a friend you don't need to talk to.
Bill Cosby *You Bet Your Life* (1993)

A friend in need is a friend in debt.   Colin M. Jarman

THE FRIEND OF MY FRIENDS ARE MY FRIENDS.
FLEMISH PROVERB

The enemy of my enemy is my enemy.   Warren Beatty *Dick Tracy* (1990)

A GIRL'S BEST FRIEND IS HER MOTHER.   AMERICAN SAYING

A girl's best friend is her mutter.   Dorothy Parker

HOW TO WIN FRIENDS AND INFLUENCE PEOPLE.
DALE CARNEGIE

Public Relations is the art of winning friends and getting people under the influence.   Anon

A MAN'S BEST FRIEND IS HIS DOG. PROVERB

A dog's best friend is his illiteracy. Ogden Nash *The Private Dining Room* (1953)

WHY, SOME OF MY BEST FRIENDS ARE WOMEN.

PHYLLIS McGINLEY *BOOK TITLE* (1940)

On anti-Semitism – God knows that I have never been that; some of
my best friends are Jews. W. Somerset Maugham *Letter* (1946)

Some of my best friends are blues. Ronnie Scott

—————— ££ FRIGHTEN ﹐﹐ ——————

**I DON'T CARE WHERE PEOPLE MAKE LOVE, SO
LONG AS THEY DON'T DO IT IN THE STREET AND
FRIGHTEN THE HORSES.** MRS PATRICK CAMPBELL Attrib.

I don't mind what the flowers do in the privacy of their own
flowerbeds or vases, so long as they don't frighten the bumble-
bees. Barry Humphries

—————— ££ FUGITIVE ﹐﹐ ——————

I AM A FUGITIVE FROM A CHAIN GANG. *FILM TITLE* (1932)

I am a Fugitive from a Daisy Chain Gang.

Dorothy Parker *New Yorker* (1933)

—————— ££ FUN ﹐﹐ ——————

**SEX IS THE MOST FUN YOU CAN HAVE WITH YOUR
CLOTHES OFF.** SAYING

Sex is the most fun I ever had without laughing. Woody Allen

Golf is the most fun you can have with your clothes on. Lee Trevino

Advertising is the most fun you can have with your clothes on.

Jerry Della Femina

Sex is the most fun you can have with the lights off. Anon

" FUNNY "

A FUNNY THING HAPPENED TO ME ON THE WAY TO THE WHITE HOUSE. ADLAI STEVENSON (1952)

Life was a funny thing that happened to me on the way to the grave.
Quentin Crisp *The Naked Civil Servant* (1968)

" FUTURE "

I HAVE SEEN THE FUTURE AND IT WORKS.
ALFRED, LORD TENNYSON *LOCKSLEY HALL* (1886)

On California – I have seen the future and it plays. John Morgan (1978)

On America – I have seen the future and it doesn't work. Philip Toynbee

I have seen the future and it's a bald-headed man from New York.
Lost In America (1985)

I have seen the future and it is being repaired. Mel Calman *The Times* (1986)

TV has seen the future . . . and it irks. *Sunday Telegraph* (1991)

I have seen the future and it's worse. Colin M. Jarman

" GAME "

IT'S A GAME OF TWO HALVES. FOOTBALL SAYING

It's a game of two teams. Peter Brackley

On the two legs of the Football League Cup Semi-finals – It's a game of four halves. Gary Lineker

It was a game of three halves. Steve Davis

Rugby Union can be a game of two fly-halves. Colin M. Jarman

" GAS "

ALL IS GAS AND GAITERS.
CHARLES DICKENS *NICHOLAS NICKLEBY* (1839)

On Pink Floyd (Rock band) – All gas and guitars. *Evening Standard* (1993)

ff GENIUS 99

GENIUS IS AN INFINITE CAPACITY FOR TAKING PAINS.
PROVERB

Genius is the capacity for evading hard work.   Elbert Hubbard

Genius has been defined as a supreme capacity for taking trouble. It might be more fitly described as a supreme capacity for getting its possessors into pains of all kinds, and keeping them therein so long as the genius remains.   Samuel Butler *Note Books* (1912)

Most human beings have an almost infinite capacity for taking things for granted.   Aldous Huxley *Themes and Variations* (1950)

Genius is an infinite capacity for taking pains. But we should still foster it, however much of an embarrassment it may be to us.
Malcolm Bradbury *Eating People is Wrong* (1959)

Genius, cried the commuter, *consists of an infinite capacity to catch trains.*   Christopher Morley

Genius is an infinite capacity for picking brains.   Anon

Talent is an infinite capacity for imitating genius.   Anon

On arriving at US Customs in New York – **I HAVE NOTHING TO DECLARE EXCEPT MY GENIUS.**   OSCAR WILDE (1882)

I have nothing to declare except my genes.   Graffiti

ff GENTLEMEN 99

GENTLEMEN PREFER BLONDES.   ANITA LOOS *BOOK TITLE* (1925)

Gentlemen prefer blondes, but they marry brunettes.   Anita Loos

It isn't that gentlemen really prefer blondes, it's just that we look dumber.   Anita Loos

More and more do gentlemen prefer gentlemen   Anita Loos

Gentlemen prefer bonds.   Andrew Mellon (1926)

It is possible that blondes also prefer gentlemen.   Mamie Van Doren

Gentlemen prefer blondes, but get what they can.   Don Herold

Gentlemen prefer blondes, due to the fact, apparently, pale hair, delicate skin and an infantile expression represent the very apex of a frailty which every man longs to violate.   Alexander King

God is a gentleman. He prefers blondes.   Joe Orton *Loot* (1965)

Gentlemen Prefer My Sister.   Stephanie Calman *Book title*

Gentlemen prefer blondes, because they get dirty quicker.   Anon

Genitals prefer blondes.   Anon

If a guy prefers blondes, it doesn't mean he's a gentleman.   Graffiti

IT TAKES THREE GENERATIONS TO MAKE A GENTLEMAN.   ROMEI *THE COURTIER'S ACADEMY* (1598)

It takes three generations or one good guess in the stock market to make a gentleman.   Anon

THE *PALL MALL GAZETTE* IS WRITTEN BY GENTLEMEN FOR GENTLEMEN. WILLIAM M. THACKERAY (c. 1850)

The *Daily Mail* is produced by office boys for office boys.   Lord Salisbury

The *Daily Express* is the paper written by the unread for the undead.   John Sweeney *Observer* (1990)

—————— ❛❛ GIFT ❜❜ ——————

DO NOT TRUST THE HORSE, TROJANS. WHATEVER IT IS, BEWARE OF GREEKS BEARING GIFTS.

VIRGIL *AENEID* (29 BC)

Beware of sheikhs sharing lifts.   Denis Nordern *My Word* (1980)

HE HAD A GOOD GIFT OF THE GAB.   SAMUEL COVIL (1695)

A dress designer merely possesses the gift of the garb.   Marvin Alisky

A shop-lifter has the gift of the grab.   Colin M. Jarman

—————— ❛❛ GIVE ❜❜ ——————

GIVE A MAN AN INCH AND HE'LL TAKE A YARD.

PUBLILIUS SYRUS (43 BC)

Give a girl an inch nowadays, and she'll make a dress of it.   Dr H. R. Pickard (1928)

Give a man a free hand and he'll run it all over you.   Mae West

Give the neighbourhood kids an inch and they'll take a yard.   Helen Castle

Give a woman an inch and she'll park a car on it.   Chief Constable E. P. White

Give a woman a job, and she grows balls.   Jack Gelber

Give someone half a page on a newspaper and they think the own the
    works.   Jeffrey Barnard

Give a woman an inch and she think she's a ruler.   Anon

Give a politician a free hand and he will put it in your pocket.   Anon

Give a pedestrian an inch and he'll take a chance.   Anon

GIVE ME A BOY UNTIL HE IS SEVEN, AND I WILL SHOW YOU A MAN.   IGNATIUS LOYOLA (c. 1540)

Give us the child for eight years, and it will be a Bolshevist forever.
                                            V. I. Lenin *Speech* (1923)

Give me a girl at an impressionable age, and she is mine for life.
                        Muriel Spark *The Prime of Miss Jean Brodie* (1961)

Give me a girl at twelve and she'll be a woman by half past. Peter Acton

GIVE ME LIBERTY OR GIVE ME DEATH.
                                        PATRICK HENRY *SPEECH* (1775)

Give me librium or give me meth.   Graffiti

—————— ❝ GLASSES ❞ ——————

LOOKING AT THE WORLD THROUGH ROSE-COLOURED GLASSES.   ANON

Stop looking at the world through rose-coloured bifocals. Dorothy Parker

I wonder if we could speak through rose-tinted spectacles?   Nick Ross

Some people don't have to look at the world through rose-coloured
    glasses – their eyes are already bloodshot.   Anon

MEN SELDOM MAKE PASSES AT GIRLS WHO WEAR GLASSES.   DOROTHY PARKER *NEWS ITEM*

Men seldom make passes at a girl who surpasses.   Franklin P. Jones

The girl who is bespectacled
Don't even get her nectacled.   Ogden Nash

Men often make passes at girls who hold glasses.   L. L. Levinson

Boy's don't make passes at female smart asses.
                            Letty C. Pogrebin *The First Ms Reader* (1972)

The types who make passes at girls who wear glasses – just so they
    can see themselves in the reflection.
                        Stephanie Calman *Gentlemen Prefer My Sister*

Men do make passes at girls who wears glasses – but it all depends
    upon their frames.   Anon optician

" GLITTERS "

ALL THAT GLITTERS IS NOT GOLD. LATIN PROVERB

All is not gold that glitters, but it is a wise child that keeps the stopper in his bottle of testing acid. O. Henry (1910)

All that glitters is sold as gold. Ogden Nash (1933)

All is not gold that glitters; all isn't garbage that smells.
Baker and Bolton *Dee to the World* (1944)

All that glisters may not be gold, but at least it contains free electrons.
J. D. Bernal *Lecture* (1960)

All that glitters isn't gold, all that doesn't glitter isn't either.
Louis Scutenaire

On Danny La Rue – It is merely proof that all that glitters is not even bronze! Sheridan Morley *The Tatler* (1970)

On Shane Gould (Australian Olympic swimming champion) – All that glitters is not Gould. US Swim Team T-shirt slogan (1972)

All that glitters is not sold. *Independent on Sunday* (1994)

" GO "

YOU GO YOUR WAY AND I'LL GO MINE. ANON SAYING

You go Uruguay and I'll go mine. Groucho Marx *Animal Crackers* (1930)

" GOD "

AND GOD SAID, LET US MAKE MAN IN OUR IMAGE, AFTER OUR LIKENESS. GENESIS 1:26 *THE BIBLE*

If God created us in His own image, we have more than reciprocated.
Voltaire

The Almighty in His infinite wisdom did not see fit to create a Frenchman in the image of Englishmen. Sir Winston Churchill (1942)

AS YOU KNOW, GOD IS USUALLY ON THE SIDE OF THE BIG SQUADRONS AGAINST THE SMALL.
COMTE DE BUSSY-RABUTIN *LETTER* (1677)

God is not on the side of the heavy battalions, but of the best shots.
Voltaire *Notebooks*

GOD DOES NOT PLAY DICE WITH THE UNIVERSE.
ALBERT EINSTEIN Attrib.

God not only plays dice, He sometimes throws the dice where they cannot be seen. Stephen Hawking *Nature* (1975)

God may not play dice with the universe, but he certainly played snooker. Anon

GOD IS DEAD, BUT LOOKING AT THE WAY MAN IS, THERE WILL PROBABLY BE CAVES FOR THOUSANDS OF YEARS TO COME IN WHICH HIS SHADOW CAN BE SEEN. FREIDRICH NIETZSCHE *THE JOYOUS SCIENCE* (1882)

God is not dead – he is alive and well and living in your heart. Christian slogan

The good news is that God is alive and well. The bad news is that he's really pissed off. Bob Hope *Playboy* (1973)

God is dead, but 50,000 social workers have risen to take his place. Dr. J. D. McCoughey (1974)

Sheila Levine is dead and living in New York. *Film title* (1975)

God is not dead – He is alive and well and working on a less ambitious project. Graffiti

God is not dead – He just couldn't find a place to park. Graffiti

Jesus is not dead – He is alive and well and signing copies of the Bible at Foyles. Graffiti

God is alive – he just doesn't want to get involved. Graffiti (1975)

After he had been horsenapped in Ireland – Shergar is alive and well and living under an assumed name. Irish Graffiti

God is dead! But don't worry, the Virgin Mary is pregnant again. Los Angeles Graffiti (1981)

On Ronald Reagan – Whatever happened to Rosemary's Baby? He's alive and living in the White House. US Graffiti

GOD IS EVERYWHERE. ANON

They say God is everywhere, and yet we always think of Him as somewhat of a recluse. Emily Dickinson

God cannot be everywhere which is why he created mothers. Anon

GOD IS LOVE. JOHN *THE BIBLE*

God is love – I dare say. But what a mischievous devil love is! Samuel Butler *Notebooks* (1912)

God is love, but get it in writing. Gypsy Rose Lee

GOD SAVES. CHURCH SLOGAN

God saves, but the physician takes the fee. Benjamin Franklin

God saves . . . but Kevin Keegan scores on the rebound. Graffiti

God saves with the Woolwich.   *Graffiti*

Jesus saves – and Moses invests.   *Graffiti*

Jesus saves, but he couldn't on my wages.   *Graffiti*

GOD SENDS US MEAT BUT THE DEVIL SENDS US COOKS.   PROVERB

God sent us women, but the devil sent them corsets.   French Proverb

God sends us friends, but the devil sends us relatives.   Anon

HOW ODD
OF GOD
TO CHOOSE
THE JEWS.   W. N. Ewer

But not so odd
As those who choose
A Jewish God
Yet spurn the Jews.   Cecil Browne

Not odd
Of God
Goyim
Annoy 'im.   Anon Jewish reply

THERE ONCE WAS A MAN WHO SAID 'GOD MUST THINK IT EXCEEDINGLY ODD, IF HE FINDS THAT THIS TREE CONTINUES TO BE WHEN THERE'S NO ONE ABOUT IN THE QUAD'.   RONALD KNOX (c. 1920)

Dear Sir, Your astonishment's odd:
I am always about in the Quad.
And that's why the tree will continue to be,
Since observed by, Yours faithfully, God.   Anon

WHAT THEREFORE GOD HATH JOINED TOGETHER, LET NO MAN PUT ASUNDER.   MATTHEW *THE BIBLE*

What God hath joined together no man ever shall put asunder: God
will take care of that.   George Bernard Shaw *Getting Married* (1908)

Law and equity are two things which God hath joined, but which man
has put asunder.   C. C. Colton

WHOM THE GODS WISH TO DESTROY THEY FIRST MAKE MAD.   PUBLILIUS SYRUS (42 BC)

When the Gods wish to punish us they answer our prayers.   Oscar Wilde

Whom the Gods which to destroy they first call promising.
Cyril Connolly *Enemies of Promise* (1938)

On Chairman Mao (Chinese political leader) – Whom the mad would destroy they first make Gods.
Bernard Levin (1967)

Whom the Gods wish to make bigots, They first deprive of humour.
James McGillis *This is Our Day*

—————— **❝ GOOD ❞** ——————

THE GOOD ENDED HAPPILY, AND THE BAD UNHAPPILY, THAT IS WHAT FICTION MEANS.
OSCAR WILDE *THE IMPORTANCE OF BEING EARNEST* (1895)

The bad ended unhappily, the good unluckily. That is what tragedy means.
Tom Stoppard *Rosencrantz and Guildenstern are Dead* (1967)

GOOD MEN ARE HARD TO FIND.
PROVERB (c. 1600)

A hard man is good to find.
Mae West

IF YOU CAN'T BE CLEVER, BE GOOD.
PALINGENIUS STELLATUS (fl. 1540) *TAURUS*

For heaven's sake be good, but if you can't be good, be careful.
A. M. Binstead *Pitcher in Paradise* (1903)

If you can't be good, belittle.
D. V. Cubberley

IT IS BETTER TO BE GOOD THAN TO BE UGLY.
OSCAR WILDE *THE PICTURE OF DORIAN GRAY* (1891)

It is better to be good than original.
Mies van der Rohe

IT WAS ALWAYS YET THE TRICK OF OUR ENGLISH NATION, IF THEY HAVE A GOOD THING, TO MAKE IT TOO COMMON.
WILLIAM SHAKESPEARE *HENRY IV Pt 2* (1592)

If it's a good thing, they'll stop making it.
Herbert Block

That's the old American way – if you've got a good thing, then overdo it.
Phil Walden

A MISS IS AS GOOD AS A MILE.
WILLIAM CAMDEN (1614)

A Ms. is a good as a male.
Feminist slogan

ONE GOOD TURN DESERVES ANOTHER.
JOHN RYLAND'S LIBRARY BULLETIN (1400)

One good turn gets most of the bed clothes.
Elaine C. Moore

READ ANY GOOD BOOKS LATELY?
ANON SAYING (c. 1910)

Booked any good Reds lately?
Anon (c. 1950)

TOO MUCH OF A GOOD THING IS GOOD FOR NOTHING. PROVERB (c. 1200)

Too much of a good thing can be wonderful. Mae West

WHAT IS NOT GOOD FOR THE SWARM IS NOT GOOD FOR THE BEE. MARCUS AURELIUS *MEDITATIONS* (c. AD 150)

What is good for the country is good for General Motors, and vice versa. Charles E. Wilson (1953)

🔊 GOVERNMENT 🔊

THE BEST GOVERNMENT IS THAT WHICH GOVERNS LEAST. JOHN L. O'SULLIVAN *THE US DEMOCRATIC REVIEW* (1837)

That best government is that which governs not at all.
Henry D. Thoreau *Civil Disobedience* (1849)

🔊 GRAPES 🔊

THE GRAPES OF WRATH. JOHN STEINBECK *BOOK TITLE* (1939)

A hangover is the wrath of grapes. *Playboy* (1965)

🔊 GREATEST 🔊

After knocking out Sonny Liston – **I AM THE GREATEST.**
CASSIUS CLAY (MUHAMMAD ALI) (1964)

On failing his army entrance exam – I said 'I was the greatest', not the smartest. Muhammad Ali

After beating Muhammad Ali – I am not the greatest. I am the latest.
Leon Spinks (1978)

🔊 GRIN 🔊

GRIN AND BEAR IT. OLD NAVAL SAYING

Don't grin, or you'll have to bear it. Ogden Nash (1938)

On tennis-player Ilie Nastase – He rarely grins and bears it. More commonly he grins, groans, shrugs, slumps, spins around, shakes his head, puffs out his cheeks, rolls on the ground and bears it. Even more common, he does all that and doesn't bear it.
Clive James *Observer*

IF GOD HAD INTENDED . . .

white to be the virginal colour, why do nuns wear black?   Dave Allen

sex to be fun, He wouldn't have included children as punishment.
                                                             Ed Bluestone

us to have group sex, I guess He'd have given us all more organs.
                                        Malcolm Bradbury *Who Do You Think You Are?*

us to be homosexual, He would have created Adam and Bruce.
                                                        Anita Bryant (1977)

us to do a thing, He should make his wishes sufficiently clear. Sensible
  people will wait until He has done this before paying much attention to Him.   Samuel Butler

us to fly, He would never have given us railways.   Michael Flanders

a round of golf to take more than three hours, He would never have
  invented Sunday lunch.   Jimmy Hill

everyone to be in bed by 10.30, He would never have provided the ten
  o'clock newscast.   Garrison Keillor

us to think with our wombs, why did He give us brains? Clare Booth Luce

us to run on pavements, He'd have given us radial toes.   Dennis Nordern

women to wear slacks, He would have constructed them differently.
                                                            Emily Post

our skeletons to be visible, He'd have put them on the outside of our
  bodies.   Elmer Rice *On bodybuilding*

Jewish women to exercise, He'd have put diamonds on the floor.
                                                           Joan Rivers

us to have children, He would have given them PVC aprons.
                                           Victoria Wood *Up to You, Porky*

us to travel tourist class, He would have made us narrower.
                                                       Martha Zimmerman

us to walk around naked, we would have been born that way.   Anon

Texans to ski, He would have made bullshit white.   Anon

us to talk more than hear, He would have given us two mouths and
  only one ear.   Anon

us to fly, He'd have given us tickets.   Graffiti

IF GOD HADN'T INTENDED . . .

man to hunt, He wouldn't have given us plaid shirts.

Johnny Carson *The Tonight Show*

us to have one night stands, He wouldn't have invented nurses.

Tony Davidson *For Him Magazine* (1993)

us to take advantage of suckers, why did He make so many of them?

Steve Martin *Leap of Faith* (1992)

man to work, He would have given him butter instead of the cow. Anon

us to write on stone walls, He would never have given us the example.

Graffiti

to give the world an enema, He wouldn't have created Benidorm. Graffiti

—————— **" GROW "** ——————

LARGE STREAMS FROM LITTLE FOUNTAINS FLOW, TALL OAKS FROM LITTLE ACORNS GROW.

DAVID EVERETT *COLUMBIAN ORATOR* (1777)

Today's mighty oak is just yesterday's nut that held its ground.

Church sign in Sussex

Great oaths from little aching corns do grow.   Anon

Great oafs from little icons grow.   Colin M. Jarman

—————— **" HABITS "** ——————

OLD HABITS DIE HARD.   J. BELKNAP *FORESTERS* (1792)

Just as old habits die hard, old hards die habits.

Kenneth Tynan *Esquire* (1968)

Old habits . . . old nuns.   Bill Cosby *You Bet Your Life* (1993)

—————— **" HALF "** ——————

HALF A LOAF IS BETTER THAN NO BREAD.

ENGLISH PROVERB

Compromise used to mean that half a loaf was better than no bread. Among modern statesmen it really seems that half a loaf is better than the whole loaf.   G. K. Chesterton

Half a life is better than no breath.   Nicolas Bentley
Half a love is better than no bride.   Frank Muir *My Word* (1974)
Half a loaf is better than no time off.   Anon

❝ HAMLET ❞

THE ARMY WITHOUT KITCHENER IS LIKE HAMLET WITHOUT THE PRINCE OF DENMARK.   *THE TIMES* (1910)

To tell the story of Coleridge without opium is to tell the story of
   Hamlet without the ghost.   Leslie Stephen

On Aneurin Bevan (Minister of Health) – A debate on the NHS
   without the Right Honourable Gentleman would be like putting on
   Hamlet with no one cast in the part of the first grave-digger.
   Iain MacLeod

On Thomas Driberg (Labour politician) – To have published an
   obituary of Tom Driberg without mentioning homosexuality would
   have been like publishing an obituary of Maria Callas without
   mentioning opera.   William Rees-Mogg *The Times* (1980)

❝ HAND ❞

THE HAND THAT ROCKS THE CRADLE IS THE HAND THAT RULES THE WORLD.
WILLIAM R. WALLACE *JOHN O'LONDON'S TREASURE TROVE* (1865)

The hand that rocks the cradle is just as liable to rock the country.
   Kin Hubbard

The hand that rocks the scales in the grocery store is the hand that
   rules the world.   Finley Peter Dunne *Mr Dooley*

You can't prevent it; it's the nature of the sex. The hand that rocks
   the cradle rocks the world, in a volcanic sense. Saki *Toys of Peace* (1916)

The hand that rocks the cradle raids the refrigerator.   Franklin P. Jones

We whose hands have rocked the cradle are now using our heads to
   rock the boat.   Wilma S. Heide

The hand that rocks the cradle may rule the world but the hand itself
   is controlled by the state.   *The Guardian* (1979)

The hand that rocks the cradle is usually attached to someone who
   isn't getting enough sleep.   Jim Fiebig

MANY HANDS MAKE LIGHT WORK.

HESIOD *WORKS AND DAYS* (c. 800 BC)

Many hands make light work, but many mouths eat up all.

H. H. Brackenridge *Modern Chivalry* (1797)

What is the use of saying 'Many hands make light work' when the same copy-book tells you that 'Too many cooks spoil the broth'?

Observer (1923)

Many Hans make Volkswagens.

K. G. Hull

Many ands make long sentences.

Colin M. Jarman

—————— " HANG " ——————

LOOKING FOR A PEG TO HANG YOUR HAT ON.

ANON SAYING

The Labour Party are looking for a peg to hang a Hatton.

Derek Hatton (1986)

[Manchester City FC] Chairman Peter Swales has now got a scapegoat to hang his hat on.

Francis Lee (1994)

————— " HAPPINESS " —————

HAPPINESS IS A THING CALLED JOE.

E. Y. HARBURG *SONG TITLE* (1942)

Happiness is a warm puppy.

Charles M. Schulz *Peanuts* (1960)

Happiness is bumping into Raquel Welch . . . very slowly.

Rowan and Martin's Laugh-In (1969)

On 'Love Story' (1970) – Happiness is a warm bed pan.

Christopher Hudson

We have lived through the era when happiness was a warm puppy, and the era when happiness was a dry martini, and now we have come to the era when happiness is knowing what your uterus looks like.

Nora Ephron *Crazy Salad* (1975)

Happiness may after all be egg-shaped, a warm puppy, the light shining in my sweetie's eye, or, like the old song, a thing called Joe.

Stanley Reynolds *Punch*

Happiness is a warm uzi.

The Distinguished Gentleman (1993)

Happiness is being single.

Bumper sticker

Happiness is egg-shaped.

Egg advert

❝ HASTE ❞

MARRY IN HASTE, AND REPENT BY LEISURE.

JOHN DAY *FESTIVALS* (1615)

I shall marry in haste and repeat at leisure. James B. Cabell

Some by experience find these words misplaced,
Marry'd at Leisure, they repent in haste.

Benjamin Franklin *Poor Richard's Almanac* (1734)

Now hatred is by far the longest pleasure;
Men love in haste, but they detest at leisure. Lord Byron *Don Juan* (1824)

They repent at leisure who marry at random. R. H. Barham (1842)

Marry in haste and repent in the suburbs. *Poor Richard Jnr's Almanac* (1906)

A manuscript is something submitted in haste and returned at leisure.

Oliver Herford

MORE HASTE, LESS SPEED. *DOUCE MS 52 no 86* (1350)

More waist, less speed. David Walters

❝ HAVE ❞

HAVE GUN, WILL TRAVEL. PERSONAL ADVERT *THE TIMES* (c. 1900)

Have handbag, will hit back back. Suzanne Moore *The Guardian* (1993)

Have wife, must travel. Anon

❝ HEAD ❞

ANYONE WHO GOES TO SEE A PSYCHIATRIST OUGHT TO HAVE HIS HEAD EXAMINED.

SAMUEL GOLDWYN Attrib.

Anyone who wants to be President should have his head examined.

Averell Harriman (1970)

HEADS I WIN, TAILS YOU LOSE. AMERICAN SAYING (c. 1830)

Heads you win, cocktails you lose. Drink-driving slogan

IF YOU CAN KEEP YOUR HEAD WHEN ALL ABOUT YOU ARE LOSING THEIRS. RUDYARD KIPLING *IF* (1902)

If you can keep your head when all about you are losing theirs, it's
just possible you haven't grasped the situation. Jean Kerr

If you can keep your head when all about you are losing theirs, you're
at the wrong end of the football pitch. Bill Munro

If you can keep your bed when all around you are losing theirs, you are probably a private patient in a NHS hospital.   Colin M. Jarman

SUCCESS HAS GONE TO HIS HEAD.   ANON SAYING

Failure has gone to his head.   Wilson Mizner

Success has gone to my stomach.   Michael Winner

Excess has gone to his head.   Anon

TWO HEADS ARE BETTER THAN ONE.
J. PALSGRAVE *LANGUE FRANCAISE* (1530)

Two heads are better than one, but not on the same body.
Bill Cosby *You Bet Your Life* (1993)

Two heads are better than one, even if one of them is a sheep's head.
Cornish proverb

Two heads aren't better than one considering the price of haircuts these days.   Anon

A kiss is a pleasant reminder that two heads are better than one.   Anon

UNEASY LIES THE HEAD THAT WEARS A CROWN.
WILLIAM SHAKESPEARE *HENRY IV Pt 2* (1592)

Uneasy lies the head that mixed hot chili, horse-radish and ice-cream at dinner.   Anon

Uneasy lies the head that ignored a phone call at 1 a.m.   Anon

Uneasy lies the tooth that wears a crown.   Colin M. Jarman

—————— " HEALTH " ——————

SMOKING CAN SERIOUSLY DAMAGE YOUR HEALTH.
GOVERNMENT HEALTH WARNING (1970)

Lawyers can seriously damage your health.   Michael Joseph (1984)

Why haven't women got labels on their foreheads saying Danger; Government Health Warning: women can seriously damage your brains, genitals, current account, confidence, razor blades and good standing among your friends.   Jeffrey Barnard *Spectator* (1984)

I swear my sons will never pick up a cue. Snooker can seriously damage your health.   Alex Higgins (1992)

Shares can seriously damage your wealth.   Anon stockbroker

Forgetting your wife's birthday can seriously damage your health. Anon

Margaret Thatcher's government should carry a Heath warning.   Anon

" HEART "

ABSENCE MAKES THE HEART GROW FONDER.

ANON *POETICAL RHAPSODY* (1602)

Absinthe makes the heart grow fonder.   Addison Mizner

Absinthe makes the tart grow fonder.   Hugh Drummond

How can you reconcile the statement that 'Absence makes the heart
grow fonder' with 'Out of sight, out of mind'?   *Observer* (1923)

Absence makes the heart go yonder.   Robert Byrne

Absence makes the heart grow fonder, but presence brings better
results.   American saying

Absence makes the mind go wander.   American saying

Absence makes the heart go wander.   Anon

Abstinence makes the head grow clearer.   Anon

Absence makes the heart grow fonder – of somebody else. Anon

CROSS MY HEART AND HOPE TO DIE.   ANON SAYING

Cross my heart and hope to eat my weight in goslings.   W. C. Fields

Cross my heart and kiss my elbow.

Audrey Hepburn *Breakfast at Tiffany's* (1961)

A FAINT HEART NEVER WON A FAIR LADY.

RICHARD TAVERNER *ERASMUS' ADAGES* (1545)

A faint heart never won a fair lay.   Sarah Harrison

A faint heart ne'er won fur, lady.   Anon

I LEFT MY HEART IN SAN FRANCISCO.

DOUGLASS CROSSMAN AND GEORGE CORY *SONG TITLE* (1954)

I left my harp in Fat Sam's Bistro.   Anon

I left my heart (and head) in El Savador.   American Graffiti

ASLEF my train in San Francisco.   Graffiti

A LIGHT PURSE MAKES A HEAVY HEART.

FRANCIS THYNNE (1600)

A light wife makes a heavy husband.   William Shakespeare

A heavy purse makes a light heart.   Ben Jonson (1629)

A light purse makes a heavy curse.   Thomas Fuller

MY HEART BLEEDS FOR YOU.   ANON SAYING

My nose bleeds for you.   Herbert Beerbohm Tree

My heart breaks for you.   Anon

THE SHORTEST ROAD TO MEN'S HEARTS IS DOWN
THEIR THROATS.   JOHN ADAMS *LETTER* (1814)

The way to an Englishman's heart is through his stomach.
Dinah M. Craik *John Halifax* (1857)

The real way to a man's stomach is through his heart. E. S. Gardner (1943)

The way to a man's heart is through his wife's belly, and don't forget
it.   Edward Albee *Who's Afraid of Virginia Woolf?* (1962)

The way to a man's heart wasn't through his stomach, it was through
an appreciation of what interested him. A. Price *Our Man in Camelot* (1975)

The way to a man's heart is through his chest.   Roseanne Barr

The way to a man's heart is through his hankie-pocket with a
bread-knife.   Jo Brand (1992)

The quickest way to to a chess player's heart is through his wallet.
William Harston (1993)

The way to a man's heart is through his penis.   Graffiti

THEIR HEART'S IN THE RIGHT PLACE.
BENJAMIN DISRAELI *THE INFERNAL MARRIAGE* (1834)

Her heart's in the right place – a pity the other thirteen stone aren't.
Anon

—————— **" HEAT "** ——————

IF YOU CAN'T STAND THE HEAT, GET OUT OF THE
KITCHEN.   MAJOR-GENERAL HARRY VAUGHAN *TIME* (1952)

(*Commonly attributed to Harry S Truman, who also said* – If you can't
stand the smell, get out of the shit-house.)

If you can't stand the heat in the kitchen, stand nearer the
refrigerator.   Bill Cosby

—————— **" HEAVEN "** ——————

OUR FATHER WHO ART IN HEAVEN, HALLOWED BE
THY NAME.   MATTHEW 6:9 *THE BIBLE*

Why should we not pray to our mother who art in heaven, as well as
to our father?   Elizabeth Cady Stanton *The Revolution* (1868)

Our Father which art in heaven, stay there; and as for us, we shall
stay on the earth.   Jacques Prevert *Pater Noster* (1946)

WHEN IT RAINS, IT RAINS PENNIES FROM HEAVEN.

JOHNNY BURKE

Pennies do not come from heaven. They have to be earned here on
earth. Margaret Thatcher

—————————— **"HELL"** ——————————

HEAVEN HAS NO RAGE LIKE LOVE TURNED TO HATRED, NOR HELL A FURY LIKE A WOMAN SCORNED.

WILLIAM CONGREVE *THE MOURNING BRIDE* (1697)

War hath no fury like a non-combatant. C. Montague (1922)

Hell hath no fury like a woman novelist. Clarissa Cushman (1941)

Hell hath no fury like an armed woman. Phoebe Taylor (1941)

There is no fury like an ex-wife searching for a new lover.
Cyril Connolly *The Unquiet Grave* (1944)

Hell hath no fury like a Liberal scorned. Dick Gregory

Hell hath no fury like a hustler with a press agent. Frank Sinatra

Hell hath no vanity like a handsome man. Coco Chanel

Hell hath no homicidal fury like a homosexual scorned.
New York Times (1967)

Hell hath no fury like a bureaucrat scorned. Milton Friedman

Hell hath no music like a woman playing second fiddle. John Patrick

Hell hath no fury like a woman's corns. L. L. Levinson

Hell hath no fury like a wallflower with a sociology degree.
Julie Burchill (1986)

Hell hath no fury like the lawyer of a woman scorned. Anon

HELL IS PAVED WITH GOOD INTENTIONS.

ST BERNARD OF CLAIRVAUX (1150)

Hell is paved with good intentions – they have their place in heaven
too. Robert Southey (1824)

Hell may be paved with good intentions, but it is assuredly hung with
Manchester cottons. Sir Charles Napier

You recollect what pavement is said to be made of good intentions. It
is made of bad intentions, too. Charles Dickens *Our Mutual Friend* (1865)

The road to ignorance is paved with good editions. George Bernard Shaw

Hell isn't merely paved with good intentions, it is walled and roofed
with them. Aldous Huxley *Time Must Have a Stop* (1944)

The road to hell is paved with works-in-progress. Philip Roth

The road to success is filled with women pushing their husbands along.   Thomas R. Dewar

Hell is paved with women's tongues.   Albe Guyon

The path of civilization is paved with tin cans.   Elbert Hubbard

On 'Super Mario Bros.' (1993) – The yellow brick road to hell is paved with bad intendoes.   Philip French *Observer*

Hell is paved with good intentions and roofed with lost opportunities.
                                                                    Anon

—————— **❝ HELP ❞** ——————

THE GODS HELP THEM THAT HELP THEMSELVES.
                                                        AESOP (c. 600 BC)

God help the rich, the poor can beg.   James Howell

God help those who help themselves.   L. L. Levinson

She who helps herself, helps herself because she keeps helping herself.
                                                        Bill Cosby (1993)

God help those who are caught helping themselves.   Anon

—————— **❝ HERE ❞** ——————

FROM HERE TO ETERNITY.   JAMES JONES *BOOK TITLE* (1951)

From here to maternity.   Blake Morrison *Independent on Sunday* (1994)

—————— **❝ HERO ❞** ——————

FROM HERO TO ZERO IS ABOUT THE AVERAGE HERO'S FATE.   EDDIE RICKENBACKER (c. 1920)

On Ben Johnson's testing positive for drugs after winning the Olympic one hundred metres gold medal – From hero to zero in 9.79 seconds.
                                            Olympic Games village Graffiti (1988)

—————— **❝ HESITATES ❞** ——————

THE WOMAN WHO DELIBERATES IS LOST.
                                                    JOSEPH ADDISON *CATO* (1713)

(*More commonly quoted as* 'He who hesitates is lost')

In Utah it is emphatically true, that he who hesitates is lost – to
Mormonism.   J. H. Beadle *Western Wilds* (1878)

She who hesitates is won.   Oscar Wilde

He who hesitates is last.   Mae West

He who hesitates is bossed.   Sonia Chapman

He who hesitates is lost – except a bachelor.   Herbert V. Prochnow

He who hesitates is not only lost, but miles from the next exit.   Anon

He who hesitates is lost; so is the woman who doesn't.   Anon

He who hesitates has lost the parking spot.   American Graffiti

" HIDE "

**NO MAN, WHEN HE HATH LIGHTED A CANDLE,
PUTTETH IT IN A SECRET PLACE, NEITHER UNDER A
BUSHEL, BUT ON A CANDLESTICK, THAT THEY
WHICH COME IN MAY SEE THE LIGHT.**

LUKE *THE BIBLE*

If one hides one's talent under a bushel one must be careful to point
out to everyone the exact bushel under which it is hidden.   Saki

" HISTORY "

HAPPY IS THE NATION WHICH HAS NO HISTORY.

ANON SAYING

The happiest women, like the happiest nations, have no history.
George Eliot *The Mill on the Floss* (1860)

HISTORY IS APT TO REPEAT ITSELF.

GEORGE ELIOT *JANET'S REPENTANCE* (1858)

History repeats itself, it is true, but history will not bear mimicry.
Augustus Jessopp *Daily Life* (1885)

History repeats itself, first as a tragedy, second as farce.   Karl Marx

History repeats itself. Historians repeat each other.   Philip Guedella

History repeats itself; that's one of the things wrong with history.
Clarence Darrow

If history repeats itself, I should think we can expect the same thing
again.   Terry Venables

Every time history repeats itself the price goes up.   Anon

Why is it nobody listens when history repeats itself?   Anon

❝ HOME ❞

HOME IS WHERE THE HEART IS.   PLINY THE ELDER (c. AD 50)

Home is where you hang yourself.   A. O. Goetz *New Yorker* (1941)

Home is where the bar is.   Craig Rice (1943)

On D.I.Y. – Home is where the hard work is.

          Dominic Murphy *The Guardian* (1993)

Home is where the art is.   Hugh Fearnley-Whittingstall *Sunday Telegraph* (1993)

Home is where the sofa is.   Sofa Workshop slogan (1994)

Home is where the hearth is.   Anon

Home is where you are buried.   Anon

Home is where the television is.   Graffiti

THE STATELY HOMES OF ENGLAND, HOW BEAUTIFUL THEY STAND! AMIDST THEIR TALL ANCESTRAL TREES, O'ER ALL THE PLEASANT LAND.

       FELICIA D. HEMANS *THE HOMES OF ENGLAND* (1826)

The Stately Homes of England, how beautiful they stand, To prove the upper classes have still the upper hand.   Noël Coward *Operette* (1938)

I am one of the stately *homos* of England.   Quentin Crisp

❝ HONESTY ❞

HONESTY IS THE BEST POLICY.

       MIGUEL DE CERVANTES *DON QUIXOTE* (1615)

I am of the opinion that, as to nations, the old maxim that honesty is the best policy is a sheer and ruinous mistake.   Washington Irving (1809)

Honesty is the best policy, but he who is governed by that maxim is not an honest man.   Richard Whatley *Detached Thoughts* (1854)

Honesty is the best policy, unless, of course, you are an exceptionally good liar.   Jerome K. Jerome

Honesty may be the best policy, because it has so little competition.

          Anon

Honesty may be the best policy, but some people are satisfied with less than the best.   Anon

Dishonesty is the best foreign policy.   Anon

❝ HOPE ❞

HE THAT LIVES UPON HOPE DIES FASTING.

ITALIAN PROVERB

He who lives upon hope, dies farting.

Anon

He that lives on hope has but a slender diet.

Anon

HOPE SPRINGS ETERNAL IN THE HUMAN BREAST.

ALEXANDER POPE *AN ESSAY ON MAN* (1732)

The fellow who said hope springs eternal in the human breast should have started probing under my vest next morning. R. L. Goldman (1942)

Hope must feel that the human breast is amazingly benevolent.

Henry H. Haskins

The hope that springs eternal springs right up your behind.

Ian Dury *This is What We Find* (1979)

Hope springs eternal in the human heart, but the spring doesn't gush as much it used to.

Anon

Dope springs eternal in the human vein.

Anon

WHERE THERE'S LIFE, THERE'S HOPE.

THEOCRITUS *IDYLLS* (300 BC)

Where there's tea, there's hope.

Sir Arthur Wing Pinero

Where there's a head, there's hope.

John Goodman *Barton Fink* (1992)

Where there's life, there's soap.

Anon

❝ HOUSE ❞

A BROTHEL IS A HOUSE OF ILL-REPUTE.

SAYING

The Vatican is a house of pill refute.

Graffiti

BUILT LIKE A BRICK SHIT HOUSE DOOR.

ANON SAYING (c. 1920)

On Natalie Wood (Actress) – She's built like a brick dolls house.

Harry Kurnitz

PEOPLE WHO LIVE IN GLASS HOUSES SHOULD NOT THROW STONES.

PROVERB

Those who live in glass houses gather no moss.

Vachel Lindsay (1914)

People who live in glass houses should be very careful.

Hugh Pentecost (1942)

People who live in glass houses have to answer the bell.   Bruce Patterson

People who live in stone houses shouldn't throw glasses.   Austin O'Malley

People who live in glass houses should pull down the blinds.
Oliver Herford

People who live in chateaux
    Shouldn't throw tomateaux.   'Beachcomber' (J. B. Morton)

People who live in large houses shouldn't know Jones.   Alan Coren

People in stucco houses shouldn't throw quiche.   Don Johnson *Miami Vice*

People who live in glass houses should undress in the basement.
American saying

People who live in glass houses make interesting neighbours.   Anon

People in glass palaces shouldn't stow thrones.   Anon

People who live in glass houses shouldn't get stoned.   Anon

THIS IS THE HOUSE THAT JACK BUILT.   NURSERY RHYME

Yankee Stadium is the house that Babe Ruth built.   Baseball saying

Ratner's is the House That Crap Built.   *The Sun* (1991)

On Hanbury Manor Golf Course designed by Jack Nicklaus Jr – The
course that Jack Jr built.
Ewen Murray *Keep Your Handicap Down* – Sky TV (1994)

The House that Crack built.   Anon

—————— **" HOW "** ——————

HOW DO I LOVE THEE? LET ME COUNT THE WAYS.
ELIZABETH BARRETT BROWNING *SONNETS FROM THE PORTUGUESE*

On David Bowie (Singer) – How do we hate thee David? Let us count
the ways.   *Melody Maker*

—————— **" HUMAN "** ——————

TO ERR IS HUMAN, TO FORGIVE, DIVINE.
ALEXANDER POPE *ESSAY ON CRITICISM* (1709)

To err is human, to repent divine, to persist devilish.
Benjamin Franklin (1742)

To eat is human, to digest, divine.   Mark Twain

To err is human – but it feels divine.   Mae West

To err is human, to forgive, infrequent.   Franklin P. Jones

On Harry S Truman (US president) – To err is Truman.

US Republican Party slogan (1948)

To err is human – to forgive, supine.

S. J. Perelman

To err is human, to forgive, takes restraint;
To forget you forgave is the mark of a saint.

Suzanne Douglass

To err is human, not to, animal.

Robert Frost *The White-tailed Hornet*

To forgive is human, to forget divine.

James Grand

To err is human, but to really foul things up requires a computer.

Paul Ehrlich *Farmer's Almanac* (1978)

To err is human. To forgive is not my policy.

Joseph Clark *Nightline* – ABC TV (1988)

To err is human, but to admit it isn't.

Herbert V. Prochnow

To err is human; to blame it on someone else is more so.

Anon

To err is human, to forgive, routine.

Anon

❝ HURT ❞

WHAT YOU DON'T KNOW WON'T HURT YOU.

GEORGE PETTIE *A PETITE PALACE OF PETTIE HIS PLEASURE* (1576)

What you do know won't hurt you much either.

Dan Bennett

What you don't owe, won't hurt you.

Anon

YOU ALWAYS HURT THE ONE YOU LOVE. ANON SAYING

You should always hurt the one you love to hate.

Anon

A boxer is a sportsman who always hurts the one he gloves.

Anon

❝ HUSH ❞

HUSH! HUSH! WHISPER WHO DARES!
CHRISTOPHER ROBIN IS SAYING HIS PRAYERS.

A. A. MILNE *WHEN WE WERE VERY YOUNG* (1927)

Hush! Hush!
Nobody cares!
Christopher Robin
Has
    Fallen
        Down-
            Stairs!

J. B. Morton *Now We Are Sick* (1931)

—————————— " IF " ——————————

**IF IFS AND ANDS WERE POTS AND PANS, THERE'D BE
NO TRADE FOR TINKERS.**   THOMAS L. PEACOCK *MANLEY* (1820)

If ifs and ands could create employment, then there would be little use
for the Minister of Labour to tinker at.   *The Times* (1924)

**IF JESUS WERE TO COME TODAY, PEOPLE WOULD
NOT EVEN CRUCIFY HIM. THEY WOULD ASK HIM TO
DINNER, AND HEAR WHAT HE HAD TO SAY, AND
MAKE FUN OF IT.**   THOMAS CARLYLE (c. 1870)

If Christ came to Sydney today He would probably be on the Hill at
cricket matches driving home the lessons of the game. One can
imagine Christ reminding the crowd that Satan was the deadliest
and most determined googly bowler of all time.   Rev. T. McVittie (1937)

If St Paul were to come back to our world in the flesh he would
become a newspaperman.   Abbe Michonneau

(*For what paper, dear God? For what paper?*   *Malcolm Muggeridge*)

If Attila the Hun were alive today, he'd be a drama critic.   Edward Albee

If Casey Stengel were alive today, he'd be spinning in his grave.

Ralph Kiner

If Robin Hood were alive today, he'd steal from the poor, because the
rich only carry credit cards.   Anon

———————— " IGNORANCE " ————————

**WHERE IGNORANCE IS BLISS, 'TIS FOLLY TO BE
WISE.**

THOMAS GRAY *ODE ON A DISTANT PROSPECT OF ETON COLLEGE* (1747)

Where ignorance is bliss, it's foolish to borrow your neighbour's
newspaper.   Kin Hubbard

Where ignorance is bliss, disillusionment, when it comes, more than
makes up for the bliss.   Lambert Jeffries

When folly is bliss, 'tis ignorance to be otherwise.   Ethel W. Mumford

Where ignorance is bliss, a little learning is a dangerous thing.

E. S. Gardner (1943)

Somebody else's ignorance is bliss.   Jack Vance *Star King*

Ignorance is not bliss – it is oblivion.   Philip Wylie *Generation of Vipers* (1942)

If ignorance is indeed bliss, it is a very low grade of the article.

Tehyi Hsieh *Chinese Epigrams* (1948)

Ignorance is a voluntary condition of bliss.   Laurence J. Peter

On Terry Dicks MP – If ignorance is bliss, he must be an extremely
    happy man. Peter Cormack

Where ignorance is bliss, stupidity invariably follows. Eric Bower

If ignorance is bliss, this is Eden. *Cheers* – NBC TV

If ignorance is bliss, why aren't there more happy people? Anon

If ignorance is bliss, what's the use of IQ tests? Anon

❝ IMITATE ❞

**GOOD PAINTERS IMITATE NATURE. BAD ONES
VOMIT IT.** MIGUEL DE CERVANTES *EL LICENCIADO VIDRIERA*

The immature poet imitates. The mature poet plagiarises. T. S. Eliot

A good composer does not imitate; he steals. Igor Stravinsky

The immature artist imitates. The mature artist steals.
Lionel Trilling *Esquire* (1962)

Artists – by definition innocent – don't steal. But they do borrow
    without giving back. Ned Rorem *Anatomy of Two Songs* (1967)

❝ INHUMANITY ❞

**MAN'S INHUMANITY TO MAN MAKES COUNTLESS
THOUSANDS MOURN!** Robert Burns *Man was Made to Mourn*

*On South African spin-bowler 'Tufty' Mann continually deceiving
    English batsman George Mann* – So what we are watching here is a
    clear case of Mann's inhumanity to Mann.
John Arlott *BBC Radio* cricket commentary (1948)

❝ INNOCENT ❞

INNOCENT UNTIL PROVED GUILTY. LEGAL MAXIM

Saints should be judged guilty until proved innocent. George Orwell (1950)

❝ INSULT ❞

THIS IS ADDING INSULT TO INJURY.
EDWARD MOORE *THE FOUNDLING* (1747)

Surtax is a tax on a tax, which is a case of adding insult to penury.
Robert Orben

X IS TO Y I

Terry Dicks MP is to the arts what James 'Bonecrusher' Smith is to lepidoptery.
                                                                    Tony Banks MP

Kenneth Clarke is to the police what King Herod is to Mothercare.
                    Mike Bennett (Chairman of Metropolitan Police Federation) (1993)

Quarry House (New DHSS headquarters) will do for Leeds what the Olympics did for Manchester.   Virginia Bottomley *Opening speech* (1993)

Eddie Waring is to Rugby League what Cyril Smith is to hang-gliding.
                                                                    Reg Bowden

Sarah Ferguson is to motherhood what her husband Prince Andrew is to nuclear physics.   Vernon Coleman *The Sun*

Tony Banks MP is a man whose contribution to the arts is about the same as Bluebeard's contribution to the institution of marriage.
                                                                    Terry Dicks MP

On the sacking of Viv Richards and Joel Garner – The Somerset County Cricket Club committee is to fair play what Colonel Gaddafi is to air safety.   Jan Foley (1986)

Jean-Claude van Damme is to Arnold Schwarzenegger what John Major is to Margaret Thatcher.   Philip French *Observer* (1993)

Michael Heseltine is to accuracy what Gary Glitter is to good taste.
                                                                    Bryan Gould (1992)

Edwina Currie is to the Conservative Party what the Bishop of Durham is to the Church of England.   Richard Holt

Nigel Lawson is to economic forecasting what Eddie the Eagle is to ski-jumping.   Neil Kinnock (1989)

They'll leave anything incompatible with their view on the cutting-room floor. *60 Minutes* [CBS TV] is to journalism what *Charley's Aunt* is to criminology.   John McNulty

A lawsuit is to ordinary life what war is to peacetime.   Jean Malcolm

Military justice is to justice what military music is to music.
                                                                    Groucho Marx

Hyperbole is to Lyndon Johnson what oxygen is to life. Bill Moyers (1969)

British Rail is to trains what Ratner's is to jewellery – crap!
                                          Reggie Nadelson *Evening Standard* (1992)

Barbra Streisand is to our histrionic aesthetics what the Vietnam war is to our politics.   John Simon

X IS TO Y II

The white bread we eat is to corn bread what Hollywood will be to
real American dramatic literature when it comes.   Sherwood Anderson

Airport: The Concorde – This trash is to movies what airline food is to
gourmet meals.   Rona Barrett (1979)

Geoff Boycott is to Australian cricket what the Boston Strangler is to
door-to-door salesmen.   Jack Birney

A cocktail is to a glass of wine what rape is to love.   Paul Claudel

Lady Caroline Lamb is to cinema what the coffee-table book is to
literature: a heavy but insubstantial irrelevance.

Roger Greenspun *New York Times* (1973)

Jackie Collins is to writing what her big sister Joan is to acting.

Campbell Grison

Pierre Corneille is to William Shakespeare as a clipped hedge is to a
forest.   Samuel Johnson

The opera is to music what a bawdy house is to a cathedral.

H. L. Mencken (1925)

I am to cricket what Dame Sybil Thorndike is to non-ferrous welding.

Frank Muir

Marcel Proust is to life what an empty orchestra pit is to music.

John Naughton *Observer* (1991)

My singing voice is to a melody what bubble-gum is to gourmet
cuisine.   Dennis Nordern

Ted Dexter is to journalism what Danny La Rue is to Rugby League.

Michael Parkinson

Hello! magazine is to serious issues what the *World Wrestling
Federation Sticker Album* is to children's literature.

Mary Riddell *Daily Mirror* (1992)

Bel Canto is to opera what pole-vaulting is to ballet, the glorification
of a performer's prowess and not a creator's imagination.

Ned Rorem *The New Republic* (1972)

The Robert Stigwood Organisation is to the cinema what Macdonald's
is to cuisine.   David Shipman

The naked truth about me is to the naked truth about Salvador Dali,
as an old ukelele in the attic is to a piano in a tree, and I mean a
piano with breasts.   James Thurber *Merry-go-Round* (1945)

Richard Clayderman is to piano playing as David Soul is to acting.

Richard Williams

" . . . ISM "

COMMUNISM IS BOLSHEVISM WITH A SHAVE.

DETROIT JOURNAL

Bolshevism is Czarism in overalls. George J. Nathan

On the assassination of Paul I, Emperor of Russia – **DESPOTISM TEMPERED BY ASSASSINATION, THAT IS OUR MAGNA CARTA.** ERNST FRIEDRICH HERBERT MUNSTER (1801)

France was long a despotism tempered by epigrams. Thomas Carlyle (1837)

Guyana: The form of government is a mild despotism tempered by sugar. Anthony Trollope *The West Indies and the Spanish Main* (1859)

A despotism tempered by dynamite. W. S. Gilbert *Utopia* (1893)

India: A despotism of office-boxes tempered by an occasional loss of keys. Lord Lytton

FASCISM IS CAPITALISM IN DECAY V. I. LENIN

Fascism is Capitalism plus murder. Upton Sinclair

On 'Tiny' Rowland and the Lonrho affair – **IT IS THE UNPLEASANT AND UNACCEPTABLE FACE OF CAPITALISM, BUT ONE SHOULD NOT SUGGEST THAT THE WHOLE OF BRITISH INDUSTRY CONSISTS OF PRACTICES OF THIS KIND.** EDWARD HEATH *SPEECH* (1973)

If you want to see the acceptable face of capitalism, go out to an oil-rig in the North Sea. Edward Heath (1974)

Of course, being called the acceptable face of capitalism would be equally insulting. 'Tiny' Rowland (1985)

On Roy Hattersley (Labour politician) – He is the acceptable face of opportunism. David Owen

Hello! magazine is the acceptable face of hypocrisy. *Cosmopolitan* (1994)

" JUDGE "

I AM SOBER AS A JUDGE.

HENRY FIELDING *DON QUIXOTE IN ENGLAND* (c. 1740)

I am as jober as a sudge. Anon

NEVER JUDGE A MAN BY HIS CLOTHES. PROVERB

Never judge a man by his clothes, but by his wife's clothes.

Thomas R. Dewar

Never judge a man by his foes, but by his friends. Colin M. Jarman

YOU CAN'T JUDGE A BOOK BY ITS COVER.

AMERICAN SAYING (c. 1920)

You can't judge a cover by its book. Fran Lebowitz

Never judge a book by a motion picture with the same title.

Los Angeles Times

Never judge a work of art by its defects. American Saying

On Judge James Pickles – You can't book a judge by his cover. Anon

Never judge a holiday resort by its postcards. Anon

❝ JUSTICE ❞

JUSTICE SHOULD NOT ONLY BE DONE, BUT SHOULD MANIFESTLY AND UNDOUBTEDLY BE SEEN TO BE DONE. LORD HEWART *KING'S BENCH REPORT* (1923)

Sex, unlike justice, should not be seen to be done. Evelyn Laye

Justice must not only be seen to be done, it has to be seen to be believed. 'Beachcomber' (J. B. Morton)

❝ KEEP ❞

KEEP THY SHOP AND THY SHOP WILL KEEP THEE.

BEN JONSON *EASTWARD HOE!* (1604)

I always say, keep a diary and someday it will keep you.

Mae West *Every Day's a Holiday* (1937)

Keep a dog and the dog will keep you. Anon

KEEP UP WITH THE JONESES.

'POP' MOMAND *CARTOON TITLE* (1910)

Keeping up with Mrs. Jones
Who also longs to rest her bones. Margaret Fishback *Dowager* (1940)

Keeping up with the Joneses was a full-time job with my mother and father. It was not until many years later when I lived alone that I realized how much cheaper it was to drag the Joneses down to my level. Quentin Crisp *The Naked Civil Servant* (1968)

You'll have the time of your life keeping up with the Joneses!

Publicity slogan for *Indiana Jones and the Last Crusade* (1989)

Keeping up with the Dow-Joneses. Wall Street saying

The family that keeps up with the Joneses doesn't always keep up with the bailiffs.   Anon

You can keep up with the Joneses, but don't overtake them on a hill.
                                                                    Anon

Who do the Joneses keep up with?   Anon

—— " KNOW " ——

EVERYTHING YOU WANTED TO KNOW ABOUT SEX, BUT WERE TOO AFRAID TO ASK. DR DAVID REUBEN *BOOK TITLE*

Everything you wanted to know about the Mafia but didn't dare ask.
                                                    Book title (1972)

FROM THE GODS COMES THE SAYING 'KNOW THYSELF'. INSCRIPTION IN THE TEMPLE OF DELPHI

In many ways the saying know thyself is lacking. Better to know other people.   Menander (300 BC)

Know thyself? If I knew myself, I'd run away.
                        Johann Wolfgang von Goethe *Conversations* (1829)

Only the shallow know themselves.   Oscar Wilde

Know thyself – but don't tell anyone.   H. F. Henrichs

HE DOESN'T KNOW HIS ARSE FROM HIS ELBOW.
                                                          ANON SAYING

He doesn't know his brass from his oboe.   Sir Henry Wood

He doesn't know his arse from a hole in the ground.
                                              American saying (1960)

Ottawa doesn't know its art from a hole in the ground.   Anon (1968)

TO KNOW HER WAS TO LOVE HER.
                                   SAMUEL ROGERS *JACQUELINE* (1814)

To really know someone is to have loved and hated him.
                                    Marcel Handeau *Erotoogie* (1935)

On movie producer Herman Mankiewicz – To know him was to like him. Not to know him was to love him.   Bert Kalmar

JOLLY MIXTURES – I

You can always judge a man by what he eats, and, therefore, a country in which there is no free lunch in no longer a free country.
Arthur 'Bugs' Baer

It's been two ends of the same coin.
Dave Bassett

On the Council of Europe – If you open that Pandora's Box you never know what Trojan 'orses will jump out.
Ernest Bevin

He can talk over the heads of the intelligentsia to grass roots level.
John Brown

I don't believe in crying over my bridge before I've eaten it.
Noel Coward *Private Lives* (1930)

You can bet your boots if the shoe was on the other foot the Americans wouldn't wear it.
Sandra Dickinson

It's another notch in the rung on the slippery slope towards anarchy.
George Gavin

So often the pendulum continues to swing with the side that has just pullled themselves out of a hole.
Tony Gubba

Manchester United are looking to Frank Stapleton to pull some magic out of the fire.
Jimmy Hill

Zivojinovic seems to be able to pull the big bullet out of the top drawer.
Mick Ingham

British Rail stabbed us in the back by blowing the talks out of the water before they even got off the ground.
Jimmy Knapp

He's coming on in fits and bounds.
Phil Liggett

We should be barking up the wrong tree to go down that road.
Professor Patrick Myndfoot

They're hanging on to their hats for grim life.
Eve Pollard

He's doing the best he can do – he's making the worst of a bad job.
Fred Trueman

It's been every colour under the rainbow.
Toyah Wilcox

What we're not going to do is set down an ideology on tablets of stone and wave it in the air.
Ian Wrigglesworth

Aberdeen are taking this bitter pill on the chin.
Anon football commentator

Once the milk has been spilt, in this sort of a case, it's very difficult to put Humpty Dumpty back on the wall again.
Anon solicitor

We should turn a deaf ear to any red herring that may be drawn across our path.
Anon

If you find you're in hot water, put your best foot forward.
Anon

❝ LACE ❞

HE WAS NOT WORTHY TO UNLOOSE THE
SHOE-LACE OF JESUS.
ROGER WILLIAMS *WRITINGS* (1676)

The blockheads talk of my being like Shakespeare – not fit to tie his
brogues.
Sir Walter Scott *Journal* (1826)

Kevin Keegan isn't fit to tie my boot-laces.
George Best

Kevin Keegan isn't fit to lace George Best's drinks.
John Roberts

❝ LAMPPOST ❞

I'M LEANING ON A LAMPPOST.
NOEL GAY *SONG TITLE* (1957)

In a little number called *Lenin on a lamppost*.
Punch

❝ LAND ❞

LAND OF HOPE AND GLORY.
A. C. BENSON *SONG TITLE* (1902)

On Fox-hunting – This land of no hope and gory pursuit.
Michael Herd *Evening Standard* (1993)

LAND OF MY FATHERS!
SIR WALTER SCOTT

On Wales – The land of my fathers. My fathers can keep it.
Dylan Thomas

OH, SAY CAN YOU SEE, BY THE DAWN'S EARLY
LIGHT . . .
'TIS THE STAR-SPANGLED BANNER; O LONG MAY IT
WAVE
O'ER THE LAND OF THE FREE, AND THE HOME OF
THE BRAVE!
FRANCIS SCOTT KEY *THE STAR-SPANGLED BANNER* (1814)

On Richard Nixon (US president) –
Oh, say can you hear on the Watergate tapes
That I gave to the Judge how I lied like a trooper?
Oh say does that flag that I've dirtied still wave?
If I play my cards right, there's some loot I can save.
George Washington's dead, like the pledge that I gave,
But if he were alive he would turn in his grave.
Roger Woddis

America is the land of the dull and the home of the literal.
Gore Vidal (1969)

Las Vegas is the land of the spree and home of the knave.
Anon

Reno is the land of the free and the home of the grave.   Anon

YOU SHALL EAT THE FAT OF THE LAND.

GENESIS 45:18 *THE BIBLE*

Fashion designers are people who live off the fad of the land.

Frank Tyger

—————————— " LAUGH " ——————————

HE LAUGHS BEST WHO LAUGHS LAST.

THE CHRISTMAS PRINCE (1607)

He laughs best whose laugh lasts.   H. W. Thompson (1940)

HE WHO LAUGHS LAST, LAUGHS LONGEST.

JOHN MASEFIELD *WIDOW IN BYE STREET* (1912)

He who laughs, lasts.   Mary Pettibone Poole

He who laughs, has not yet heard the bad news.   Bertolt Brecht

He who laughs last is the one who intended to tell the joke himself.

The Lion

He who laughs last may laugh best, but soon gets a reputation for
  being slow.   Anon

LAUGH, AND THE WORLD LAUGHS WITH YOU.
WEEP, AND YOU WEEP ALONE.

Ella Wheeler Wilcox *New York Sun* (1883)

Laugh, and the world laughs with you; Weep, and they give you the
  laugh.   O. Henry *Trimmed Lamp* (1907)

Laugh and the world laughs with you. Snore and you sleep alone.

Anthony Burgess

Cough and the world coughs with you. Fart and you stand alone.

Trevor Griffiths

One of the silliest of all proverbs is 'Laugh and the world laughs with
  you' – certainly, so far as books are concerned. There is nothing
  more individual than taste in humour.   *Daily Telegraph* (1979)

On the size of his nose – Laugh and the world laughs with you. Sneeze
  and it's goodbye Seattle.   Steve Martin *Roxanne* (1987)

Knock, and the world knocks with you; Boost, and you boost alone.

American Saying

Laugh and the world laughs with you; cry and the other guy has an
  even better sob story.   Anon

Laugh and the world laughs with you; think and you will almost die
  of loneliness.   Anon

LAUGH? I THOUGHT I WAS GOING TO DIE.

ANON SAYING (1880)

Laugh? I thought my pants would never dry. Canadian saying

Laugh? I nearly fell off my wife. Anon

—— **" LAURELS "** ——

REST ON ONE'S LAURELS.

ANON

If you rest on your laurels, they tend to become wreaths. Harry Secombe

Holding a grudge is a form of resting on one's quarrels. Vida Shiffrer

—— **" LEAD "** ——

AND LEAD US NOT INTO TEMPTATION, BUT DELIVER US FROM EVIL.

MATTHEW 6:13 *THE BIBLE*

Lord lead us not into temptation. Just show us where to find it. Anon

YOU CAN LEAD A HORSE TO WATER BUT YOU CAN'T MAKE HIM DRINK.

PROVERB

You can lead a man up to the university but you can't make him think. Finley Peter Dunne

After being asked to make a sentence with the word 'horticulture' – You can lead a horticulture but you can't make her think. Dorothy Parker

A bad salesman tries to take the horse to water and make him drink. Good salesmen make the horse thirsty.

Gabriel M. Siegel *Sales Lecture* (1984)

You can lead a herring to water, but you have to walk really fast or they die. Betty White *The Golden Girls*

On actor Jean-Claude van Damme – You can take a horse to water but you can't make him act. James Cameron-Wilson *Film Review* (1993)

—— **" LEGEND "** ——

FLORENCE NIGHTINGALE IS A LEGEND IN HER OWN LIFETIME.

LYTTON STRACHEY

On Clifford Makins (Journalist) – A legend in his own lunchtime.

Christopher Wordsworth

On Jake LaMotta (Middleweight boxer) – I'd like to introduce a man
who is a legacy in his own lifetime.   Dennis Rappaport

On Glenn Miller (Band-leader) – He became a legend in his own
lifetime because of his early death.   Nicholas Parsons

On Reggie and Ronnie Kray (Gangsters) – Legends in their own life
sentence.   Robert King

On Barry Hearn (Sports promoter) – He is still a legend in his own
mind.   Mickey Duff

On Michael Foot (Labour leader) – A leg end in his own lifetime. Anon

A legend in his own part-time.   Anon

A legend in her own flexitime.   Anon

A legend in her own night-time.   Anon

—————— " LET " ——————

NATURE AND NATURE'S LAWS LAY HID IN NIGHT: GOD SAID, *LET NEWTON BE!* AND ALL WAS LIGHT.

Alexander Pope *Epitaph for Isaac Newton* (1727)

It did not last: the devil howling *Ho!*
Let Einstein be! restored the status quo.   Sir John Squire

—————— " LIBERAL " ——————

A LIBERAL IS A CONSERVATIVE WHO'S BEEN MUGGED BY REALITY.   ANON

A conservative is a liberal who got mugged the night before.
Frank Rizzo (1972)

A liberal is a conservative who has been arrested.
Tom Wolfe *Bonfire of the Vanities* (1987)

—————— " LIE " ——————

FATHER, I CANNOT TELL A LIE, I DID IT WITH MY LITTLE HATCHET.   GEORGE WASHINGTON Attrib.

Washington could not tell a lie; Nixon could not tell the truth; Reagan
cannot tell the difference.   Mort Sahl

I cannot tell a lie, not even when I hear one.   John K. Bangs

FIGURES DON'T LIE.   ENGLISH PROVERB (c. 1800)

Figures don't lie, but liars figure.   Anon

THERE ARE THREE KINDS OF LIE: LIES, DAMNED LIES AND STATISTICS.
BENJAMIN DISRAELI *AUTOBIOGRAPHY*

Truth, damned truth and statistics.　　　*Mail on Sunday* (1993)

On the Malaysian Pergau dam contract row – Lies, dam lies and
politicians.　　　Richard Ingram *Observer* (1994)

" LIES "

MY BONNY LIES OVER THE OCEAN.
ANON (1882)

My daddy lies over the ocean, my mummy lies over the sea,
My daddy lies over my mummy, and that's how they got little me.
Anon

" LIFE "

HUMAN LIFE IS JUST A WAY OF FILLING IN TIME UNTIL THE ARRIVAL OF DEATH OR SANTA CLAUS.
ERIC BERNE *GAMES PEOPLE PLAY* (1964)

Life is just a way of filling in between Bank Holidays.
Peter Young *Jazz Fm* (1993)

IN THE MIDST OF LIFE WE ARE IN DEATH.
THE BOOK OF COMMON PRAYER (1662)

In the midst of life we are in debt.　　　Ethel Mumford

IS THERE LIFE AFTER DEATH?
ANON SAYING

Is there life before death?　　　Anon

Is there life after Wogan?　　　Graffiti (1984)

IT'S NOT THE MEN IN MY LIFE THAT COUNT; IT'S THE LIFE IN MY MEN.
MAE WEST

It's not the year in your life but the life in your year that counts.
Adlai Stevenson

LIFE BEGINS AT FORTY. THIS IS THE REVOLUTIONARY OUTCOME OF THE NEW ERA.
W. B. PITKIN *LIFE BEGINS AT FORTY* (1932)

Life begins at eight-thirty.　　　Emlyn Williams *Play title*

Life begins at forty, but so do lumbago, bad eyesight,
arthritis . . .　　　Anon

Life doesn't begin at forty for the driver who went eighty when he was twenty. Anon

Life begins at 40mph. Bumper sticker

LIFE IS A BOWL OF CHERRIES. SONG TITLE (1934)

If life is a bowl of cherries, what am I doing in the pits?
Erma Brombeck *Book title* (1978)

LIFE IS A GAME OF DICE. TERENCE *ADELPHI* (160 BC)

Life is a game of cards. Everytime you think you've got the ace you find you haven't. Peter Cheyney *A Trap for Bellamy* (1941)

Life is a game of errors; he who makes the fewest wins.
J. H. Rhoades *Jonathan's Apothegms* (1942)

LIFE IS JUST ONE DAMNED THING AFTER ANOTHER.
ELBERT HUBBARD *A THOUSAND AND ONE EPIGRAMS*

It's not true that life is one damn thing after another – it's one damn thing over and over. Edna St Vincent Millay

LIFE ISN'T ALL BEER AND SKITTLES.
T. C. HALIBURTON *NATURE AND HUMAN NATURE* (1855)

Life isn't all beer and skittles, but beer and skittles, or something better of the same sort, must form part of every Englishman's education. Thomas Hughes *Tom Brown's Schooldays* (1857)

Life ain't all beer and skittles. and more's the pity; but what's the odds, so long as you're happy. George du Maurier *Trilby* (1894)

Life isn't all beer and skittles; some of us haven't touched a skittle in years. Anon

LIFE IS TOO SHORT, THE CRAFT SO LONG TO LEARN. HIPPOCRATES (c. 350 BC)

Life is too short to learn German. Richard Porson

Life is too short to be small. Benjamin Disraeli

Life is too short for chess. Henry J. Byron *Our Boys* (1875)

Art is long and life is short: here is evidently the explanation of a Brahms symphony. Edward Lorne *Fanfare* (1922)

Life is too short – avoid causing yawns. Elinor Glyn

Life is too short to do anything for oneself that one cannot pay others to do for one. W. Somerset Maugham *The Summing Up*

Life is too short, live it up. Nikita Khrushchev (1958)

Our motto: Life is too short to stuff a mushroom.
Shirley Conran *Superwoman*

LIFE'S A BITCH, THEN YOU DIE. ANON

Life's a bitch. Now so am I. Jack Nicholson *Batman Returns* (1992)

Life's a beach, then you fry. Anon

Life's a bitch, then you diet. Anon

Life's a bitch . . . it had to be a woman! Graffiti

THE LIGHT AT THE END OF THE TUNNEL.

STANLEY BALDWIN

We don't see the end of the tunnel, but I must say I don't think it is darker than it was a year ago, and in some ways lighter.

John F. Kennedy (1962)

On the Vietnam War – The cave at the end of the tunnel.

National Lampoon (1975)

Politicians are people who, when they see the light at the end of the tunnel, order more tunnel. Sir John Quinton *Money* (1989)

On the British economy – The light at the end of the tunnel turned out to be someone with a torch . . . and the batteries are running down. *Cosmopolitan* (1994)

The light at the end of the tunnel is usually an approaching train.

Dunne's Law

Because of the present economic climate, the light at the end of the tunnel will be switched off at weekends. London Underground Graffiti

—————— **" LIGHTNING "** ——————

LIGHTNING NEVER STRIKES TWICE IN THE SAME PLACE, NOR CANNON BALLS EITHER, I PRESUME.

P. H. MYERS *PRISONER OF BORDER* (1857)

Examiners, like lightning, never strike twice in the same place.

Richard Gordon

—————— **" LION "** ——————

THE WOLF SHALL ALSO DWELL WITH THE LAMB, AND THE LEOPARD SHALL LIE DOWN WITH THE KID; AND THE CALF AND THE YOUNG LION AND THE FATLING TOGETHER. ISAIAH *THE BIBLE*

No absolute is going to make the lion lie down with the lamb unless the lamb is inside. D. H. Lawrence

The lion and the calf shall lie down together, but the calf won't get
much sleep.
Woody Allen

MARCH COMES IN LIKE A LION, AND GOES OUT LIKE A LAMB.
PROVERB

On Frederic March (Actor) – March comes in like a lion and goes out
like a ham.
Frank S. Nugent *New York Times*

—————— " LITTLE " ——————

A LITTLE LEARNING IS A DANGEROUS THING.
ALEXANDER POPE *ESSAY ON CRITICISM* (1711)

A little learning is a dangerous thing, and a great deal cannot be
hammer'd into the heads of vulgar men.
George Colman Jnr (1830)

If a little learning is dangerous, where is the man who has so much as
to be out of danger.
Thomas Huxley *Science and Culture* (1881)

A little sincerity is a dangerous thing and a great deal of it is
absolutely fatal.
Oscar Wilde *The Critic as Artist*

A little science might possibly be a dangerous thing.
Agatha Christie *Easy to Kill* (1939)

A little learning is a dangerous thing, but a lot of ignorance is just as
bad.
Bob Edwards

A little learning is a dangerous thing. That's why so many persons
don't fool with it.
Dan Kidney

A little knowledge is a dangerous thing, but no knowledge is positively
fatal.
Lambert Jeffries

A little learning is a dangerous thing to one who does not mistake it
for a great deal.
William A. White

If a little learning was a dangerous thing, a lot was lethal.
Tom Sharpe *Porterhouse Blue* (1974)

A little burning is a dangerous thing.
Anti-cigarette slogan

A little woman is a dangerous thing.
Anon

A little yearning is a dangerous thing.
Graffiti

A little Lenin was a dangerous thing.
Colin M. Jarman

—————— " LOOK " ——————

LOOK BEFORE YOU LEAP.
PROVERB

When you feel tempted to marry . . . look twice before you leap.
Charlotte Brontë *Shirley* (1849)

STOP, LOOK, LISTEN.   US RAILWAY SIGN

Stop. look, lessen.   Diet slogan

❝ LORD ❞

THE LORD GAVE, AND THE LORD HATH TAKEN AWAY.   JOB 1:21 *BIBLE*

The Lord giveth and the landlord taketh away.   John W. Raper

❝ LOSE ❞

TO LOSE ONE PARENT, MR WORTHING, MAY BE REGARDED AS A MISFORTUNE; TO LOSE BOTH LOOKS LIKE CARELESSNESS.

OSCAR WILDE *THE IMPORTANCE OF BEING EARNEST* (1895)

To lose a lover or even a husband or two during the course of one's life can be vexing. But to lose one's teeth is a catastrophe.

Hugh Wheeler *A Little Night Music*

❝ LOT ❞

A POLICEMAN'S LOT IS NOT A HAPPY ONE.

W. S. GILBERT *THE PIRATES OF PENZANCE* (1879)

A woman's lot is not a nappy one.   Graffiti

❝ LOUDER ❞

ACTIONS SPEAK LOUDER THAN WORDS.

JOHN PYM *SPEECH* (1628)

Facts speak louder than words, and, under certain circumstances, louder than oaths.   Alexander Hamilton *Papers* (1792)

Actions lie louder than words.   Carolyn Wells

Facts speak louder than statistics.   Sir Geoffrey Streatfield (1950)

Actions speak louder than words, but not so often.

Farmers' Almanac (1966)

Actions speak louder than words – and speak fewer lies.   Anon

Actions speak louder than words and are apt to be misquoted.   Anon

JOLLY MIXTURES – II

Michael Heseltine should come out of the woodwork, stop waving his plastic chickens about, run up his flag up the flag-pole and see who salutes.
                                                    John Banham (1990)

You have reached the turning point on a voyage of no return.
                                                    Simon Bates

He went down like a sack of potatoes, then made a meal of it.
                                                    Trevor Brooking

The Americans have sowed the seed, and now they have reaped the whirlwind.   Sebastian Coe

Businessmen should stand or fall on their own two feet.   Edwina Currie

He's the one rotten apple who turns out to be the good egg.
                                                    William Feaver

An egghead is one who stands firmly on both feet in the air on both sides of an issue.   Homer Ferguson (1954)

I suppose if you let this genie out of the bottle, you'd get, to continue the allusion, a whole lot of butterflies out of Pandora's Box.
                                                    Pru Goward

I went up the greasy pole of politics step by step.   Michael Heseltine

It's like a game of chess: all the cards are thrown in the air, the board's turned over and you're in a whole new ball game.
                                                    Michael Howard

It's unlucky to walk under a black cat.   Max Kauffmann

After banging your head against a brick wall for long enough you'd think that some of it would rub off.   Alex Murphy

The run of the ball is not always in our court at the moment.   Phil Neal

I think I can scotch that one on the head right away.   Sir Jeremy Thomas

We are sitting on a powder-keg that could explode in our faces at any time.   Bishop Desmond Tutu

On the Falklands War – This is the run-up to the big match which should be a walk-over.   Rear Admiral Sandy Woodward (1982)

The hurdles we had to climb were traditionally untrodden . . . so we were blazing new trails all the time.   Anon power expert

Necessity is the mother of strange bedfellows.   Anon

" LOVE "

ALL MANKIND LOVE A LOVER.
R. W. EMERSON

All the world loves a lover, but not while the love-making is going on.
Elbert Hubbard

All the world loves a lover, but it shows more consideration toward the expectant father.
J. P. McEvoy

All the world loves a lover, except those who are waiting to use the telephone.
Anon

THE COURSE OF TRUE LOVE NEVER DID RUN SMOOTH.
WILLIAM SHAKESPEARE *A MIDSUMMER NIGHT'S DREAM* (1596)

The course of true love never did run smooth, nor the course of anything else that belongs to man.
William Wirt *Letters* (1833)

The course of true anything never does run smooth.
Samuel Butler

If there is any country where the course of true love may be expected to run smooth, it is America.
Harriet Martineau

The course of true love never runs – it stops and it parks.
Anon

GREATER LOVE HATH NO MAN THAN THIS, THAT A MAN LAY DOWN HIS LIFE FOR HIS FRIENDS.
JOHN 15:13 *THE BIBLE*

Greater luck hath no man than this, that he lay down his wife at the right moment.
Samuel Butler

Greater love than this, he said, no man hath that a man lay down his wife for a friend.
James Joyce *Ulysses* (1922)

Greater love hath no man than this, that he should lay down his cheque-book for his life.
Anthony Boucher (1942)

On Harold MacMillan (who had made sweeping changes to his cabinet) – Greater love hath no man than this, that he lay down his friends for his life.
Jeremy Thorpe

All the kids of draft age can count on Spiro Agnew to lay down your life for his country.
Vietnam Graffiti (1971)

I AM WILLING TO LOVE ALL MANKIND.
ANON

I am willing to love all mankind except an American.
Samuel Johnson

It is easier to love all mankind than to love one's neighbour.
Eric Hoffer

I am willing to love mankind – it's people I can't stand.
Charles M. Schultz *Peanuts*

IT IS LOVE, LOVE, LOVE, THAT MAKES THE WORLD GO ROUND.
DUMERSON AND SEGUR *POPULAR SONGS OF FRANCE* (1851)

It's said that love makes the world go round. The announcement lacks verification. It's the wind from the dinner horn that does it.

O. Henry *Brandur Magazine* (1902)

It may be love that makes the world go round, but it's spinsters who oil the wheels. Ellen Abb

Love doesn't make the world go round. Love is what makes the ride worth-while. Franklin P. Jones

Money makes the world go round. Fred Ebb *Money* 1972

Money has done more than make the sports world go round, it has made it spin off its axis. Gary Pomerantz

A love of fashion makes the economy go round. Liz Tilberis (1987)

Love makes the world go round, but so does too much red pepper in the chili. Anon

Love makes the world go round, with that worried expression. Anon

It's gossip that makes the word go round. Colin M. Jarman

LOVE CONQUERS ALL THINGS. VIRGIL (c. 30 BC)

Love conquers all things except poverty and toothache. Mae West

LOVE IS A MANY-SPLENDOURED THING.

HAN SUYIN *BOOK TITLE*

Love is a many gendered thing. Graffiti

LOVE IS BLIND. THEOCRITUS (c. 250 BC)

Though love is blind, yet 'tis not for want of eyes. Proverb (1500)

Love is blind; friendship closes its eyes. French proverb

Love is blind, but hatred is as bad. Thomas Fuller (1732)

Love is not really blind – the bandage is never so tight but that it can peep. Elbert Hubbard

Love is not blind; that is the last thing it is. Love is bound; and the more it is bound the less it is blind. G. K. Chesterton

Love is said to be blind, but I know lots of fellows in love who can see twice as much in their sweethearts as I can. Josh Billings

Love is blind but marriage restores the sight. Georg Lichtenberg

On divorce – Love is a wonderful thing but as long as it's blind I will never be out of a job. Justice Selby (1968)

Love is blind and your cane is pink. Serge Gainsbourg (1983)

Love may be blind, but jealousy sees too much. Anon

Never kiss your lover at the garden gate, love is blind, but the neighbours ain't. Anon

Love is blond. Anon

LOVE THY NEIGHBOUR. THALES (c. 600 BC)

I love my neighbour as myself, and to avoid coveting my neighbour's wife I desire to be coveted by her – which you know is another thing. William Congreve

Do not love your neighbour as yourself. If you are on good terms with yourself it is an impertinence; if on bad, an injury.
G. B. Shaw *Man and Superman* (1903)

Love thy neighbour as thyself – but choose your neighbourhood.
Louise Beal

Love thy enemy – it'll drive him nuts. Eleanor Doan

Leave thy neighbour. Alliance + Leicester Building Society mortgage advert (1993)

Love thy neighbour – but don't get caught. Graffiti

WHEN POVERTY COMES IN AT THE DOOR, LOVE FLIES OUT THE WINDOW. PROVERB

When mother-in-law comes in at the front door, love flies out the window. Helen Rowland

When love comes in the door, money flies innuendo. Groucho Marx

WHO EVER LOVED, THAT DID NOT LOVE AT FIRST SIGHT? CHRISTOPHER MARLOWE *HERO AND LEANDER* (1598)

Love at first sight is possible, but it is always well to take a second look. Anon

Love a first sight is the greatest time-saving in the world. Anon

Love at first sight usually ends in divorce at first slight. Anon

—————— **" MAD "** ——————

DON'T GET MAD, GET EVEN. AMERICAN SAYING

Don't get mad, get angry. Edwina Currie

The American adage 'don't get mad, get even' doesn't apply to Norman Tebbitt – he gets mad *and* even. Observer

—————— **" MAGNIFIQUE "** ——————

On the Charge of the Light Brigade – **C'EST MAGNIFIQUE, MAIS CE N'EST PAS LA GUERRE.** (*It's magnificient, but it's not war*) MARSHAL PIERRE BOSQUET (1854)

On margarine – C'est magnifique, mais ce n'est pas le beurre. *(It's magnificient, but it's not butter)*   Punch (c. 1915)

To a taxi-driver who had taken him to St Lazare, instead of the Riviera – C'est magnifique, mais ce n'est pas la gare. (*It's magnificient, but it's not the station*)   Anon

—————— **"MAN"** ——————

A MAN IS AS OLD AS HE'S FEELING. A WOMAN AS OLD AS SHE LOOKS.

MORTIMER COLLINS *THE UNKNOWN QUANTITY* (1855)

I believe that a person is as old as his habits.

Gelett Burgess *Look Eleven Years Younger* (1937)

A woman is as old as she looks to a man that likes to look at her.

Finley Peter Dunne

A man is as old as the woman he feels.   Groucho Marx

A man is as old as his arteries.   Dr Thomas Sydenham

A woman is as young as her knees.   Mary Quant

A MAN IS KNOWN BY THE COMPANY HE KEEPS.

MILES COVERDALE *CHRISTIAN STATE OF MATRIMONY* (1541)

A man is known by the company he organises.   Ambrose Bierce

A lady is known by the product she endorses.   Ogden Nash

A man is known by the silence he keeps.   Oliver Herford

A man is known by the company he keeps . . . out of.   A. Craig

People knew a man by the company he kept, but they generally knew a woman by the man who kept her.   Lisa Alther *Kinflicks* (1976)

A company is judged by the President it keeps.   James Herbert

A careful driver is know by the fenders he keeps.   American saying

A woman is known by the company with which she sleeps.   Anon

MAN IS THE ONLY ANIMAL OF PREY THAT IS SOCIABLE. EVERY ONE OF US PREYS UPON HIS NEIGHBOUR, AND YET WE HERD TOGETHER.

JOHN GAY (c. 1700)

Man is the only animal that is hungry with his belly full.

H. Gates *Proceedings* (1776)

Man is the only animal that makes bargains; no other animal does this – no dog exchanges bones with another.   Adam Smith

Man is the only animal that blushes – or needs to.

Mark Twain *Following the Equator* (1897)

Man is the only animal that has the true religion – several of them.

Mark Twain

Man is the only animal that can remain on friendly terms with the victims he intends to eat until he eats them.   Samuel Butler

Man is the only animal that plays poker.   Don Herold

Man is the only animal that can be a fool.   Holbrook Jackson

Man is the only animal that eats when he is not hungry, drinks when he is not thirsty, and makes love at all seasons.   Anon

Man is the only animal that laughs. He is also the only man that has a legislature.   Anon

Man is the only animal that apologises – or needs to.   Anon

READING MAKETH A FULL MAN.

FRANCIS BACON *OF STUDIES* (1625)

Bacon maketh a fat man.   Graffiti

WHATSOEVER A MAN SOWETH, THAT SHALL HE ALSO REAP.

GALATIANS 6:7 *THE BIBLE*

Whatsoever a man shall smoke, so he shall reek.   *Reader's Digest* (1949)

Whatsoever a man shall rip, he shall also sew.   L. L. Levinson

—————— **"MARRIAGE"** ——————

LET ME NOT TO THE MARRIAGE OF TRUE MINDS ADMIT IMPEDIMENTS.   WILLIAM SHAKESPEARE *SONNETS*

Let me not to the marriage of true swine admit impediments

Wendy Cope *Making Cocoa for Kingsley Amis*

MARRIAGE IS A GREAT INSTITUTION.   ANON SAYING

Marriage is a great institution – but I'm not ready for an institution yet.   Mae West

Marriage is a great institution – no family should be without it.

Bob Hope

A MARRIAGE IS MADE IN HEAVEN AND PERFORMED ON EARTH.   WILLIAM PAINTER *PALACE OF PLEASURE* (1567)

They tell me that marriage is made in Heaven, I tell them, so are thunder and lightning.   Clint Eastwood

Marriages have to be made in heaven because they never work on earth.   Lucy Ellman *Observer* (1993)

A marriage is made in heaven and deformed on Earth. Anon

MARRIAGE IS NOT A BED OF ROSES. R. L. STEVENSON

Marriage is not all bed and breakfast. R. Coulson *Reflections*

MARRIAGE IS THE ONLY ADVENTURE OPEN TO THE COWARDLY. VOLTAIRE Attrib.

Marriage is the only adventure open to the cowardly, a certain man
   says. He made a mistake; you have to be a hero to face the pains
   and disappointments. Clifford Odets (1938)

—————————— **&& MEEK ""** ——————————

BLESSED ARE THE MEEK: FOR THEY SHALL INHERIT THE EARTH. MATTHEW 3:5 *THE BIBLE*

The English are mentioned in the Bible: Blessed are the meek for they
   shall inherit the earth. Mark Twain

Blessed are the meek for they shall inherit the dearth. J. B. Opdyke (1912)

It's going to be interesting to see how long the meek can keep the
   earth when they inherit it. Kin Hubbard *Abe Martin's Sayings* (1915)

Blessed are the young, for they shall inherit the National Debt.
   Herbert Hoover

The meek shall disinherit the earth. Horace Gregory (1935)

We have the highest authority for believing that the meek shall inherit
   the Earth; though I have never found any particular corroboration
   of this aphorism in the records of Somerset House. F. E. Smith

Let the meek inherit the earth, they have it coming to them.
   James Thurber

Pity the meek, for they shall inherit the earth. Don Marquis

The meek shall inherit the earth, but not its mineral rights. J. Paul Getty

The meek do not inherit the earth unless they are prepared to fight for
   their meekness. Harold J. Laski

The meek shall inherit the earth, but it's the grumpy who get
   promoted. *M*A*S*H*

Unless pollution is controlled, the muck shall inherit the earth.
   Conservation slogan

The meek shall inherit the earth, if that's all right with the rest of you?
   Anon

When the meek shall inherit the earth, they will also inherit a good
   many instalment payments from those who weren't so meek. Anon

Blessed are the meek, for they shall inhibit the earth. Graffiti

The meek shall inherit the earth, they're too weak to refuse. Graffiti
The earth shall inherit the meek. Graffiti

—— **" MESS "** ——

HERE'S ANOTHER FINE MESS YOU'VE GOT US INTO, STANLEY.
OLIVER HARDY *CATCHPHRASE* (c. 1925)

On the Falklands War – Here's another fine mess you've got us into, Port Stanley. Graffiti (1982)

—— **" MICE "** ——

THE BEST LAID SCHEMES O' MICE AN' MEN GANG AFT A-GLEY.
ROBERT BURNS *TO A MOUSE*

How many mice had Burns studied before deciding that their best-laid schemes gang aft a-gley? Auberon Waugh

The best laid plans of mice and men are filed away – somewhere. Graffiti

—— **" MILK "** ——

IT'S NO USE CRYING OVER SPILT MILK.
J. HOWELL *PROVERBS* (1659)

It's no use crying over spilt milk, because all the forces of the universe were bent on spilling it. W. Somerset Maugham *Of Human Bondage* (1915)

There's no use crying over spilt milk, it only makes it salty for the cat.
Anon

YET I DO FEAR THY NATURE;
IT IS TOO FULL OF THE MILK OF HUMAN KINDNESS
TO CATCH THE NEAREST WAY.
WILLIAM SHAKESPEARE *MACBETH* (1606)

The cheerful clatter of Sir James Barrie's cans as he went around with the milk of human kindness. Philip Guedella

Charity is the sterilized milk of human kindness. Oliver Herford

Professional charity is the milk of human blindness. Thomas L. Masson

I am full of the milk of human kindness, damn it. My trouble is that it gets clotted so easily. Gilbert Harding

—————— " MIND " ——————

**YOU MUST MIND YOUR P's AND Q's WITH HIM, I CAN
TELL YOU.** HANNAH COWLEY *WHO'S THE DUPE?* (1779)

The Chinese are a prudent people – they mind their peas and cues.
George D. Prentice (1860)

—————— " MIRROR " ——————

TO HOLD, AS IT WERE, THE MIRROR UP TO NATURE.
WILLIAM SHAKESPEARE *HAMLET* (1602)

He holds the mirror up to Nietzcshe. Philip Guedella

—————— " MISTAKES " ——————

**DOCTORS BURY THEIR MISTAKES. LAWYERS HANG
THEM. JOURNALISTS PUT THEIRS ON THE FRONT
PAGE.** ANON

A doctor can bury his mistakes, but an architect can only advise his
client to plant vines. Frank Lloyd Wright

Doctors may bury their mistakes, but cleaners sweep theirs under the
carpet, manicurists just file them away and cattle-ranchers lose
theirs in the rounding up. Colin M. Jarman

—————— " MONEY " ——————

MONEY CAN'T BUY LOVE. ANON SAYING

Money cannot buy the fuel of love but is excellent kindling. W. H. Auden

Money cannot buy love, but it makes shopping for it a lot easier.
Bo Derek

MONEY CAN'T BUY YOU HAPPINESS.
PHILIP MASSINGER *THE UNNATURAL COMBAT* (1619)

Money can't buy you happiness. People with $10 million are no
happier than people with $9 million. Hobart Brown

Among the things money can't buy are the things it used to.
Max Kauffmann

While money can't buy everything, it certainly puts you in a great bargaining position.   A. H. Berzen *Wall Street Journal*

Money can't buy friends, but you can get a better class of enemy.
          Spike Milligan

People say money can't buy you happiness, but I have always thought that if you have enough money, you can have a key made.
          Joan Rivers

The whole idea is to deliver what money cannot buy.   Bruce Springsteen

Money can't buy you happiness, but at least you can afford to rent it for the evening.   Madonna

Whoever said money can't buy happiness didn't know where to shop.
          Anon

Money can't buy you happiness, unless you spend it on someone else.
          Anon

Money can't buy you happiness, but it helps to be unhappy in comfort.   Anon

MONEY ISN'T EVERYTHING.   ANON SAYING

Money isn't everything, not always.   Eugene O'Neill *Marco Millions* (1927)

Money isn't everything – it's a long way ahead of what comes next.
          Sir Edmund Stockdale

Money isn't everything – according to those who have it.   Malcolm Forbes

Money isn't everything – usually it isn't even enough.   Anon

MONEY TALKS.   APHRA BEHN Attrib. (c. 1670)

When money talks, the truth keeps silent.   Russian proverb

That money talks I'll not deny.

I heard it once – say *Goodbye*.   Richard Armour

When money talks, there are few interruptions.   Herbert V. Prochnow

Money doesn't talk, it swears.   Bob Dylan *It's Alright Ma*

Inflation is when money still talks, but in an apologetic tone.
          Colonel MacKay *Daily Telegraph*

Money talks – bullshit walks.   American saying

Money talks but pound for pound its voice is getting weaker.   Anon

Money used to talk, now it just goes without saying.   Anon

ONE FOR THE MONEY, TWO FOR THE SHOW.
          CARL PERKINS *BLUE SUEDE SHOES* (1956)

One for the money, Two for the show, Three to get ready, Four to go. But after you get home it's ten for the babysitter.   Anon

REMEMBER THAT TIME IS MONEY.
          BENJAMIN FRANKLIN *PAPERS* (1748)

Time is a waste of money.   Oscar Wilde *Phrases for the Young* (1894)

Time is money – says the vulgarest saw known to any age or people.
Turn it round about, and you get a precious truth – money is time.
George Gissing *Henry Ryecroft* (1903)

Time is money, especially overtime.   Evan Esar

Dime is money, as the Dutchman said.   American saying

Crime is money.   Anon

" MONKEYS "

**IF AN INFINITE NUMBER OF MONKEYS SAT TYPING
AT AN INFINITE NUMBER OF TYPEWRITERS, THEY
WOULD PRODUCE THE COMPLETE WORKS OF
WILLIAM SHAKESPEARE.**   ANON

If an infinite number of monkeys sat typing at an infinite number of
typewriters, the smell in the room would be unbearable.
Anon John Hopkins University professor

" MONTH "

IT MAY LAST A MONTH OF SUNDAYS.
FREDERICK MARRYAT *NEWTON FORSTER* (1832)

The salad course nowadays seems to be a month of sundaes.
Ogden Nash (1935)

" MOTHER "

EXPERIENCE IS THE MOTHER OF WISDOM.
THOMAS DRAXE (1616)

If experience is the mother of wisdom, history must be an improving
teacher.   *American Museum* (1788)

NECESSITY IS THE MOTHER OF INVENTION.
PLATO (c. 400 BC)

Necessity may be the mother of lucrative invention, but it is the death
of poetical invention.   William Shenstone *Detached Thoughts* (1763)

Necessity is the mother of taking chances.   Mark Twain

A guilty conscience is the mother of invention.   Carolyn Wells

Necessity is the mother of futile dodges.   Alfred N. Whitehead

Invention is the mother of necessity. Thorstein Veblen

Necessity is the smotherer of convention. Lambert Jeffries

If necessity is the mother of invention, what was papa doing?
Ruth Weekley

Necessity is the mother of invention, and peril is the father. Anon

What relation is a loaf of bread to a locomotive? – Mother!
Bread is a necessity while a locomotive is an invention, thus –
necessity is the mother of invention! Arsenio Hall (1986)

Obesity is the mother of invention. Anon

Necessity is the mother of convention. Graffiti

❝ MOULD ❞

NATURE MADE HIM, AND THEN BROKE THE MOULD.
LUDOVICO ARIOSTO *ORLANDO FURIOSO* (1532)

Just before they made S. J. Perelman, they broke the mould.
Dorothy Parker

❝ MOUNTAIN ❞

CLIMB EVERY MOUNTAIN, FORD EVERY STREAM.
RODGERS AND HAMMERSTEIN *THE SOUND OF MUSIC*

Climb every mountain, ford every burn,
Suffer a thrombosis, end up in an urn. Arthur Marshall

When asked why he wished to climb Everest – **BECAUSE IT IS
THERE.** GEORGE MALLORY (1923)

They say they climb mountains because they are there. I wonder if it
would astound them to know that the very same reason is why the
rest of us go around them S. Omar Barker

A man shovels snow for the same reason he climbs a mountain –
because it's there! Nathan Nielsen

On why Prince Philip married Queen Elizabeth – Because she was
there. Richard Ingrams *Private Eye*

Some men try to climb mountains, because they are there; others try
to date them. Anon

" MOUTH "

OUT OF THE MOUTHS OF VERY BABES AND SUCKLINGS HAST THOU ORDAINED STRENGTH.

PSALMS *THE BIBLE*

Out of the mouths of babes do we learn.

Rudyard Kipling *Puck of Pook's Hill* (1906)

Out of the mouths of babes . . . usually when you've got your best suit on. G. Baxter

Out of the mouths of babes come things you wouldn't want your neighbours to hear. Mrs H. Meade

PUT YOUR MONEY WHERE YOUR MOUTH IS.

ANON SAYING

Put your money where your need is. Madeleine E. Cohen (1988)

The NUPE candidate should put her voice where her mouth is.

Derek Hatton

In recent years, the Designer Dyke has become a common urban type. Some of them actually do put honey where their mouth is.

Julie Burchill *Absolute Filth* (1993)

YOU NEVER OPEN YOUR MOUTH BUT TO PUT YOUR FOOT IN IT. P. W. JOYCE *ENGLISH AS WE SPEAK* (1910)

A bore is somebody who opens his mouth and puts his feats in it.

Henry Ford

Dopedentology is the art of putting one's foot in one's mouth.

Prince Philip

" MURDER "

MURDER MOST FOUL. WILLIAM SHAKESPEARE *HAMLET* (1602)

On Woody Allen's 'Manhattan Murder Mystery' (1993) – Murder most fun. Steve Vinberg *Modern Review*

MURDER WILL OUT, CERTAIN, IT WILL NOT FAIL.

GEOFFREY CHAUCER *THE PRIORESS'S TALE* (1386)

Murderers will out. Ogden Nash (1935)

Vanity, like murder, will out. Hannah Cowley *Belle's Stratagem*

Contact lenses will out . . . usually at the worst possible moment.

Colin M. Jarman

"MUSIC"

IF MUSIC BE THE FOOD OF LOVE, PLAY ON.
WILLIAM SHAKESPEARE *TWELFTH NIGHT* (1602)

If music be the breakfast food of love, kindly do not disturb until lunch time. James Agee *Agee on Film*

If music be the food of love, why do The Eurythmics insist on serving up spam and chips all the time? Pauline (1989)

If music be the food of love, why don't rabbits sing? D. J. Hurst

If music be the food of love, let's have a bite of your maracas. Graffiti

MUSIC HAS CHARMS TO SOOTHE A SAVAGE BREAST.
WILLIAM CONGREVE *THE MOURNING BRIDE* (1697)

(*More commonly,* 'Music has charms to soothe a savage beast')

Music hath charm to soothe a savage beast – but I'd try a revolver first. Josh Billings

YOU HIT THE NAIL ON THE HEAD.
M. STANBRIDGE (1508)

Mr [William] Gladstone showed in argument a knack for hitting the nail almost on the head. James Bryce *Contemporary Biography* (1903)

Stanley Baldwin always hits the nail on the head, but it doesn't go in any further. G. M. Young

"MYSTERIOUS"

GOD MOVES IN A MYSTERIOUS WAY HIS WONDERS TO PERFORM.
WILLIAM COWPER *OLNEY HYMNS* (1779)

Abscond. To *move* in a mysterious way, commonly with the property of another. Ambrose Bierce *The Devil's Dictionary* (1911)

God moves in a mysterious way His blunders to perform.
Running to Paradise (1943)

"NAKED"

THE NAKED APE.
DESMOND MORRIS *BOOK TITLE* (1967)

The Naked Civil Servant. Quentin Crisp *Book title* (1968)

On John Major (Prime Minister) – The knackered civil servant.
Rory Bremner (1993)

NATIONALITIES

One American, a businessman
Two Americans, a market
Three Americans, a cartel.   Anon

One Dutchman, a citizen
Two Dutchmen, a bicycle club
Three Dutchmen, irrigation.   Anon

One Englishman, a bore
Two Englishmen, a club
Three Englishmen, an empire.   Anon

One Frenchman, a lover
Two Frenchmen, an affair
Three Frenchmen, a menage.   Anon

One German makes a philosopher
Two a public meeting
Three a war.   Robert MacDonald *Summit Conference* (1982)

One German, a burgher
Two Germans, a beer-parlour
Three Germans, an army.   Anon

One Irishman, a drinker
Two Irishmen, a fight
Three Irishmen, partition.   Anon

One Italian, a tenor
Two Italians, a duet
Three Italians, an opera.   Anon

One Japanese, a gardener
Two Japanese, a cult
Three Japanese, electronics.   Anon

One Russian is an anarchist
Two Russians are a chess game.
Three Russians are a revolution.
Four Russians are the Budapest String Quartet.   Jascha Heifetz

Three Spaniards,
Four opinions.   Spanish proverb

One Swiss, one Swiss
Two Swiss, two Swiss
Three Swiss, three Swiss.   Anon

"NATION"

TO FOUND A GREAT EMPIRE FOR THE SOLE PURPOSE OF RAISING UP A PEOPLE OF CUSTOMERS, MAY AT FIRST SIGHT APPEAR A PROJECT FIT ONLY FOR A NATION OF SHOPKEEPERS.

ADAM SMITH *WEALTH OF NATIONS* (1776)

(Generally attributed to Napoleon Bonaparte)

It is beginning to be hinted that we are a nation of amateurs.

Archibald Primrose, 5th Earl of Rosebery

Maybe Napoleon was wrong when he said we were a nation of shopkeepers. Today England looked like a nation of goalkeepers.

Tom Stoppard *Professional Foul* (1977)

Americans are a nation of salesmen just as the English are a nation of small shopkeepers.   Ruth Rendell *Put on thy Cunning* (1981)

We're no longer a nation of shopkeepers, we're a nation of cowboys.

Kirsty MacColl (1989)

We are a nation of shoplifters.   Anon

"NEVER"

BETTER LATE THAN NEVER.   DIONYSUS (25 BC)

Better late than never, but better never late.   C. H. Spurgeon (1885)

Better late than never, as Noah remarked to the zebra, who had understood that passengers arrived in alphabetical order.

Bert L. Taylor *The So-called Human Race* (1921)

It is better to copulate than never.   Robert Heinlein

Better relate than never.   Anon

It is better latent than never.   Graffiti

YOU ARE NEVER TOO OLD TO LEARN WHAT IS ALWAYS NECESSARY TO KNOW.

SIR ROGER L'ESTRANGE *THE OBSERVATOR* (1681)

A woman is never too old to yearn.   Addison Mizner

You're never too old to stop learning.   Ian Botham

One is never too old to learn something stupid.   Anon

NEVER IN THE FIELD OF HUMAN CONFLICT WAS SO MUCH OWED BY SO MANY TO SO FEW.

SIR WINSTON CHURCHILL *SPEECH* (1940)

On miniskirts – Never in the history of fashion has so little material been raised so high to reveal so much that needs to be covered so badly.   Cecil Beaton (1969)

On boxing managers – Never in the ring of human conflict have so few taken so much from so many.   Saoul Mamby

On supersonic flight – Never before in history would so many have been disturbed by so few.   Bo Lundburg

Never in the history of human credit has so much been owed by so many to so few.   Margaret Thatcher (1975)

── **❝ NEWS ❞** ──

Motto of the 'New York Times' – **ALL THE NEWS THAT'S FIT TO PRINT.**   ADOLPH S. OCHS

All the news that fits, we print.   Howard Dietz

BAD NEWS TRAVELS FAST.   PLUTARCH (c. AD 100)

Bad news travels first.   Anon

NO NEWS IS GOOD NEWS.   ITALIAN PROVERB

No news is good news; no journalists is even better.   Nicolas Bentley

Good news is no news.   Lambert Jeffries

No news is preferable.   Fran Lebowitz *Metropolitan Life* (1978)

── **❝ NICE ❞** ──

On Mel Ott (Baseball player) – **NICE GUYS FINISH LAST.**
                                                LEO DUROCHER (1946)

Nice guys begin to accept defeat.   Stuart Storey

Last guys don't finish nice.   Stanley Keeley

The art of being a successful football coach seems to owe more to the axiom that nice guys finish last, than to the theory that contented cows give better milk.   George Frazier IV *Esquire* (1968)

Gary Lineker has proved that nice guys can come first.   Peter Shilton

Nice guys may finish last. But they finish.   Washington D.C. traffic sign

Nice girls don't furnish lust.   Anon

NATIONAL TRAITS

Love in France is a comedy; in England a tragedy; in Italy an opera
seria; and in Germany a melodrama.   Lady Blessington

An Irishman fights before he reasons, a Scotchman reasons before he
fights, an Englishman is not particular as to the order of prefer-
ence, but will do either to accomodate his customers.
                                        Charles C. Colton *Lacon* (1820)

A modern general has said that the best troops would be as follows:
an Irishman half drunk, a Scotchman half starved, and an Englishman with his belly full.   Charles C. Colton (1820)

Heaven is an English policeman, a French cook, a German engineer,
an Italian lover and everything organised by the Swiss.
Hell is an English cook, a French engineer, a German policeman, a
Swiss lover and everything organised by an Italian.   John Elliott (1986)

Three smallest books: British Book of Space Achievement, Italian War
Heroes and the Scottish Giftbook.   Robin Mckie *Observer* (1993)

Frustrate a Frenchman, he will drink himself to death; an Irishman,
will die of angry hypertension; a Dane, he will shoot himself; an
American, he will get drunk, shoot you, then establish a million
dollar aid program for your relatives. Then he will die of an ulcer.
                                        Stanley Rudin (1963)

Britain has football hooligans, Germany has neo-Nazis, France has
farmers.   *The Times* (1992)

Eat in Poland, drink in Hungary, sleep in Germany, and make love in
Italy.   Polish proverb

The six most dangerous things in the world:
A drunken Irishman with a broken whiskey bottle,
An Italian with an education,
A Mexican with a driver's licence,
A Jew with authority,
A Greek with tennis shoes, and
A Frenchman with a chipped tooth   Anon

The five shortest books in the world:
Jewish Business Ethics,
Italian War Heroes,
The Complete History of German Humour,
Great British Lovers, and
Who's Who in Puerto Rico   Anon

Minimum qualifications required of an overseas employee in a
   multi-national company:
Precision of an Italian,
Generosity of a Dutchman,
Humility of a German,
Charm of a Soviet,
Linguistic Ability of an American,
Ready wit of a Scandiavian,
Internationalism of an Englishman,
Road Manners of a Frenchman,
Diplomacy of an Israeli,
Culture of an Australian,
Decisiveness of a Japanese,
Impulsiveness of a Chinaman,
Gaiety of a Swiss,
Intelligence of an Irishman,
Urgency of a Spaniard.   Anon

" NIGHT "

GHOULIES AND GHOSTIES AND LONG LEGGETY BEASTIES AND THINGS THAT GO BUMP IN THE NIGHT.
CORNISH PRAYER

Women who do not use contraception grow plump in the night.   Anon

THE MORNING AFTER THE NIGHT BEFORE. ANON SAYING

Mourning after the night before.   Anti-Drink and Drive slogan (1993)

A honeymoon is the morning after the knot before.   Anon

A hangover – the moaning after the night before.   Colin M. Jarman

THE NIGHT OF THE LONG KNIVES.
ADOLF HITLER *SPEECH* (1934)

On Margaret Thatcher's cabinet reshuffle – The night of the long
   hat-pin.   Anon (1981)

TENDER IS THE NIGHT.   JOHN KEATS *ODE TO A NIGHTINGALE* (1819)

Legal tender is the night.   Graffiti

" NONSENSE "

**ALL MIMSY WERE THE BOROGROVES,
AND THE MOME RATHS OUTGRABE.**

LEWIS CARROLL *THROUGH THE LOOKING GLASS* (1871)

The mome rath isn't born that could outgrabe me.   Nicol Williamson (1972)

SUPERCALIFRAGILISTICEXPIALIDOCIOUS.   *MARY POPPINS*

Soup, a cauli, fridge, elastic, eggs, peas, halitosis.

Frank Muir *My Word* (1973)

" NOTHING "

MUCH ADO ABOUT NOTHING.

WILLIAM SHAKESPEARE *PLAY TITLE* (1599)

No man thinks there is much ado about nothing when the ado is
about himself.   Anthony Trollope

Proposed newspaper headline on an eventful scoreless football game –
Much ado about nothing-nothing.   John MacAdam

Sex for a fat man is much a do about puffing.

Jackie Gleason *Playboy* (1986)

A sneeze is much achoo about nothing.   Anon

NOTHING LASTS FOREVER.   PROVERB

Nothing lasts forever, not even a bath.   Anon

NURSE RE-RHYMES

GEORGIE PORGIE PUDDING AND PIE . . .

Georgie Porgie pudding and pie
Kissed the girls and made them cry;
When the boys came out to play
He kissed them too, he's funny that way.   Anon

HALF A POUND OF TUPPENY RICE, HALF A POUND OF TREACLE . . .

Half a pound of Mandy Rice, half a pound of Keeler,
Neither girl is very nice, everybody feel her.   Anon

HUMPTY DUMPTY . . .   ANON (1750)

Humpty Dumpty sat on a wall
Humpty Dumpty had a great fall
All the King's horses and all the King's men
Had scrambled eggs for the next six weeks.   Anon

Humpty Dumpty sat on a wall,
Humpty busted, and that'll be all.   O. Henry (1909)

JACK AND JILL WENT UP THE HILL . . .

Jack and Jill went up the hill
To fetch pail of water.
I don't know what they did up there,
But they came down with a daughter.   Anon

JACK BE NIMBLE . . .

Jack is nimble and Jack is quick
But Jill prefers the Candlestick.   Anon

Jack is nimble and Jack is quick
Jack jumped over the candlestick;
Silly boy, should have jumped higher,
Goodness gracious, great balls of fire!   Anon

JACK SPRAT . . .   JOHN CLARKE (1639)

Jack Sprat could eat no fat.
His wife could eat no lean.
A real pair of neurotics.   Jack Sharkey

JINGLE BELLS . . .

Jingle Bells, Jingle Bells,
Jingle all the way,
The family runs up great big bills
That Dad will have to pay.   Herbert V. Prochnow

LITTLE BO PEEP . . .

Little Bo Peep
Has lost her sheep
And thinks they may be roaming.
They haven't fled;
They've all dropped dead
From nerve gas in Wyoming.   Frank Jacobs *Mad Magazine* (1972)

MARY HAD A LITTLE LAMB . . .   SARAH J. HALE (1830)

Mary had a little lamb –
The midwife fainted.   Leonard Rossiter

Mary had a little lamb,
She kept it as a pet
But when the price of meat went up,
She ate the little get.   Anon

Mary had a little lamb,
The butcher chopped it dead.
She took it to school next day,
Between two chunks of bread.   Anon

Mary had a little lamb,
The doctor was surprised
But when Old MacDonald had a farm
He couldn't believe his eyes.   Graffiti

ONE, TWO, BUCKLE MY SHOE . . .   ANON (1805)

One, Two, Three.
Buckle my shoe.   George S. Kaufman

RING A RING A ROSES . . .

Ring around a neutron
A pocketful of protons
A fission, a fusion
We all fall down   Anon

Ring a ring of B.T.
A pocketful of profits.   Anon

SHE BATHED WITH ROSES RED AND VIOLETS BLEW AND ALL THE SWEETEST FLOWERS THAT IN THE FOREST GREW.
EDMUND SPENSER *THE FAERIE QUEENE* (1590)

Roses are red, Violets are blue.
I'm Schizophrenic and so am I.
Frank Crow

Roses are red, Violets are blue
Please spare a penny for a starving poet.
Private Eye

Roses are red, violets are blue
I'm dyslexic, and os era oyu.
Spike Milligan

Roses are red, Pansies are gay
If it wasn't for women, we'd all be that way.
Anon

Roses are reddish, Violets are bluish
If it wasn't for Jesus, we'd all be Jewish.
Anon

Rose's are red, Violet's are blue and mine are white.
Anon

Roses are red, Violets are blue
Why can't black be beautiful, too?
Anon

Neuroses are red
Depression is blue
I'm schizophrenic
How about you?
Anon

SIX A SONG OF SIXPENCE . . .
ANON (c. 1744)

Sing a song of sixpence, a pocket full of rye,
Four and twenty blackbirds baked in a pie.
When the pie was opened the birds burst into song –
These bloody micro-ovens are always going wrong.
Lambert Jeffries

—— ❝ OBEYED ❞ ——

ORDERS MUST BE OBEYED AT ALL TIMES. ANON SAYING
Hors d'oeuvres must be obeyed at all times.
John Cleese *Fawlty Towers* – BBC TV

" OBSCENITY "

OBSCENITY IS WHAT HAPPENS TO SHOCK SOME ELDERLY AND IGNORANT MAGISTRATE.

BERTRAND RUSSELL *LOOK* (1973)

. . . while pornography is what gives a judge an erection. Graffiti

" OFFER "

I'LL MAKE HIM AN OFFER HE CAN'T REFUSE.

MARIO PUZO *THE GODFATHER* (1969)

An office you can't refuse. Tyne & Wear Development Corporation advert (1993)

Make him a coffee he can't refuse. Anon

" OIL "

WE BURN THE MIDNIGHT OIL.

FRANCES QUARLES *EMBLEMS* (1635)

I've been burning the midday oil. Ronald Reagan (1986)

" ONCE "

ONCE A KNIGHT, EVER A KNIGHT.

J. MABBE *ALEMAN'S GUZMAN* (1622)

On refusing to join a second orgy – Once a philosopher, always a
   pervert. Voltaire

Once a knight, always a knight. Once a prostitute, always a prostitute
   is a fair mode of argument – at least among politicians.

Humphrey Marshall *Kentucky* (1824)

Once a night, every night, you're doing alright. Anon

Twice a night, dead at forty. Anon

" ONE "

ALL FOR ONE AND ONE FOR ALL.

ALEXANDER DUMAS *THE THREE MUSKETEERS* (1844)

One for all and all for me – me for you and three for five and six for
   a quarter. Groucho Marx *The Cocoanuts* (1929)

On refusing to work for any other film director except Josef von
   Sternberg – Von for all and all for Von. Marlene Dietrich

All for one, and I'm the one. American saying

ONE AND ONE MAKES TWO. MATHEMATICAL PRECEPT

We used to think that if we knew one, we knew two, because one and
   one are two. We are finding that we must learn a great deal more
   about *and*. Sir Arthur Eddington *The Harvest of a Quiet Eye*

In the arithmetic of love, one plus one equals everything and two
   minus one equals nothing. Mignon McLaughlin

—— ❝ OPPORTUNITY ❞ ——

OPPORTUNITY SELDOM KNOCKS TWICE

NATHANIEL BAILEY *ETYMOLOGICAL DICTIONARY* (1736)

Though opportunity may knock twice, there was no guarantee that it
   would knock as insistently as now. J. Bingham *Brock* (1981)

When opportunity knocks nowadays, you find that your door has to
   be unlocked, the chain removed and the alarm disconnected. Anon

The trouble with opportunity is that it only knocks. Temptation kicks
   the door down. Anon

Opportunity doesn't knock now, it rings the phone and asks you a
   silly question. Anon

—— ❝ OUT ❞ ——

OUT OF SIGHT, OUT OF MIND. ENGLISH PROVERB (c. 1250)

Out of sight, out of mind when translated into Russian by a computer
   then back again, became Invisible maniac. Arthur Calder-Marshall

—— ❝ OVER ❞ ——

THE GAME AIN'T OVER TILL IT'S OVER.

LAWRENCE 'YOGI' BERRA

The rodeo ain't over till the bull rider rides. Ralph Carpenter (1978)

The opera ain't over till the fat lady sings. Dan Cook (1978)

The golf game isn't over till the last putt drops. Cary Middlecoff

On Francis F. Coppola directing 'The Godfather III' – It ain't over till
the Fat Man directs. *L.A. Magazine* (1990)

The game ain't over till Milli Vanilli sings.

Green Bay Packers American football banner (1990)

The opera ain't over till the fat lady eats. Anon

The opera ain't over till the fat lady sweats. Anon

❝ OYSTER ❞

WHY, THEN THE WORLD IS MY OYSTER.

WILLIAM SHAKESPEARE *THE MERRY WIVES OF WINDSOR* (1598)

The world is your lobster. Leon Griffiths

❝ PAINT ❞

PABLO PICASSO PAINTS BY NUMBERS. GRAFFITI

[J. W. T.] Turner paints by nimbus. Graffiti

❝ PAY ❞

HYPOCRISY IS THE HOMAGE THAT VICE PAYS TO VIRTUE.

FRANCOIS DUC DE LA ROCHEFOUCAULD *REFLECTIONS* (1678)

Caricature is the tribute that mediocrity pays to genius. Oscar Wilde

Fraud is the homage that force pays to reason. Charles P. Curtis

LIVE NOW, PAY LATER. ANON SAYING

Buy now, pay later. Anon

Die now, pay later. Graffiti

❝ PEN ❞

THE PEN IS MIGHTIER THAN THE SWORD.

ROBERT BURTON *ANATOMY OF MELANCHOLY* (1621)

The pen is noisier than the sword. Phyllis McGinley (1940)

The pen is mightier than the sword, but no match for a gun.

Leiber and Stoller

Don't forget, the penis is mightier than the sword. Screamin' Jay Hawkins

The pen is mightier than the sword and considerably easier to write
with. Marty Feldman

The man who said the pen is mightier than the sword ought to have
tried reading *The Mill on the Floss* to Motor Mechanics.
Tom Sharpe *Wilt* (1976)

The oil-can is mightier than the sword. Everett Dirksen

This is not the age of pamphleteers. It is the age of engineers. The
spark-gap is mightier than the pen. Lancelot Hogben

On Jean-Marie Le Pen (French politician) – Power of Le Pen proves
mightier than the soured. *Sunday Telegraph* (1991)

THE PEN IS THE TONGUE OF THE MIND.

MIGUEL DE CERVANTES *DON QUIXOTE* (1615)

The pen is the tongue of the hand. Henry Ward Beecher (1887)

The penis is the tongue of the erotic mind. Anon

❝ PENNY ❞

IN FOR A PENNY, IN FOR A POUND.

THOMAS RAVENSCROFT *THE CANTERBURY GUESTS* (1695)

In for a mill, in for a million. Ralph W. Emerson *Essays* (1844)

In for a penne, out for a pound. Bella Pasta special offer (1993)

A PENNY FOR YOUR THOUGHTS.

JOHN HEYWOOD *PROVERBS* (1546)

Why is it a penny for your thoughts, but you have to put your two
cents in? Somebody's making a penny! Steve Wright

A penny for your faults. Anon

A PENNY SAVED IS A PENNY EARNED.

GEORGE HERBERT *OUTLANDISH PROVERBS* (1640)

A penny saved is a penny to squander.
Ambrose Bierce *The Devil's Dictionary* (1911)

A penny saved is a penny earned. But that was before sales tax was
invented. Anon

" PEOPLE "

DEMOCRACY, THAT IS, A GOVERNMENT OF ALL THE PEOPLE, BY ALL THE PEOPLE, AND FOR ALL THE PEOPLE. THEODORE PARKER *SPEECH* (1850)

Democracy means simply the bludgeoning of the people, by the people, for the people. Oscar Wilde *The Soul of Man Under Socialism* (1895)

The democratic system which we call the government of the people, for the people, by the people, and to hell with the people.
Michael Arlen (1939)

The American Government is a rule of the people by the people for the boss. Austin O'Malley

" PLAGUE "

A CLERGYMAN WHO IS ALSO A MAN OF BUSINESS SHOULD BE AVOIDED LIKE THE PLAGUE.
ST JEROME (c. 300)

Clichés should be avoided like the plague. Arthur Christiansen

" POACHERS "

OLD POACHERS MAKE THE BEST GAMEKEEPERS.
PROVERB

Old poachers make the best soup.
Anon contestant *Fifteen-to-One* – Channel 4 (1991)

" POLITICS "

POLITICS IS THE ART OF THE POSSIBLE, THE ATTAINABLE, THE ART OF THE NEXT BEST THING.
OTTO VON BISMARCK (1867)

If politics is the art of the possible, research is surely the art of the soluble. Sir Peter Medawar *The Art of the Soluble* (1967)

Politics is not the art of the possible. It consists of choosing between the disastrous and the unpalatable.
J. K. Galbraith *Ambassador's Journal* (1969)

Politics is the art of postponing decisions until they are no longer relevant. Henri Queuille

Politics is the art of turning the possible into the improbable. Anon

—— 🍀 PORTRAIT 🍀 ——

PORTRAIT OF THE ARTIST AS A YOUNG MAN.
JAMES JOYCE *BOOK TITLE* (1916)

Portrait of the artist as a young dog. Dylan Thomas *Book title* (1940)

—— 🍀 POT 🍀 ——

PUTTING A QUART INTO A PINT POT. *Daily News* (1896)

A quart may not go into a pint pot, but my feet had to go into these boots. W. Foley *Child in Forest* (1974)

It's a pity somebody cannot put a bullet in a Pol Pot. Anon

—— 🍀 POUR 🍀 ——

IT NEVER RAINS BUT IT POURS. THOMAS GRAY *LETTER* (1771)

It never rains monkeys but it pours gorillas. Langdon Mitchell (1906)

Pandemonium did not reign, it poured. John K. Bangs

On Tom Cruise – When he pours, he reigns.
Movie publicity slogan for *Cocktail* (1989)

—— 🍀 POVERTY 🍀 ——

POVERTY IS NO DISGRACE TO A MAN, BUT IT IS CONFOUNDEDLY INCONVENIENT.
SYDNEY SMITH *WIT AND WISDOM* (1900)

Poverty is no disgrace, but name anything in its favour. Anon

Poverty is no disgrace, but ignorance is. Anon

"POWER "

POWER WITHOUT RESPONSIBILITY – THE PREROGATIVE OF THE HARLOT THROUGH THE AGES.
RUDYARD KIPLING

The House of Lords, an illusion to which I have never been able to subscribe – responsibility without power, the prerogative of the eunuch throughout the ages. Tom Stoppard *Lord Malquist and Mr Moon* (1966)

The power to get other people to do things has been the prerogative of the harlot throughout the ages – and of the manager.
Katharine Whitehorn (1985)

"PRESIDENT "

I TRUST THE SENTIMENTS AND OPINIONS ARE CORRECT; I HAD RATHER BE RIGHT THAN PRESIDENT.
HENRY CLAY SPEECH (1839)

Henry Clay said 'I would rather be right than be president.' He doesn't have to worry. He'll never be either. Congressman Reed

Henry Clay said 'I would rather be right than be president.' This was the sourest grape since Aesop originated his fable. Irving Stone

On Franklin D. Roosevelt (US president) – I'd rather be right than be Roosevelt. Heywood Broun

Women would rather be right than be reasonable.
Ogden Nash Who Understands Who Anyway? (1940)

While I'd rather be right than President, at any time I'm ready to be both. Norman M. Thomas

WHEN I WAS A BOY, I WAS TOLD THAT ANYBODY COULD BECOME PRESIDENT, I'M BEGINNING TO BELIEVE IT.
CLARENCE DARROW

Harry Truman proves the old adage that any man can become President of the United States. Norman M. Thomas

In America any boy may become President, but I just dismissed it as a normal risk that any red-blooded American boy has to take.
Adlai Stevenson (1952)

Any kid can grow up to be President – or kill one.
Kenneth Hurren Mail on Sunday (1992)

❝ PRESS ❞

IF I RESCUED A CHILD FROM DROWNING, THE PRESS WOULD NO DOUBT HEADLINE THE STORY, 'BENN GRABS CHILD'. TONY BENN (1975)

If I blow my nose the *Daily Mail* headline would say I am trying to spread germ warfare. Ken Livingstone (1992)

❝ PROOF ❞

THE PROOF OF THE PUDDING IS IN THE EATING.
MIGUEL DE CERVANTES *DON QUIXOTE* (1615)

A golfing trophy is merely proof of the putting. Shelby Friedman

❝ PUBLIC ❞

THE PUBLIC BE DAMNED. WILLIAM VANDERBILT

I realized that Vanderbilt had been all wrong when he said, 'The public be damned!' What he ought to have said was 'The public be dumb!' A. Merritt (1928)

The public is damned, but it attends to matters itself.
Meditation in Wall Street (1940)

❝ PUBLISH ❞

In response to a blackmail letter over memoirs – **PUBLISH AND BE DAMNED!** DUKE OF WELLINGTON Attrib.

Our Motto is: Publish and be sued. Richard Ingrams *Private Eye*

My motto is: Publish and be absent. Peter Cook *Private Eye*

❝ PUNCTUALITY ❞

PUNCTUALITY IS THE VIRTUE OF PRINCES.
MARIA EDGEWORTH *HELEN* (1834)

Punctuality is the virtue of the bored. Evelyn Waugh *Diaries* (1962)

PROPORTION

Idealism increases in direct proportion to one's distance from the
problem.   John Galsworthy

The probability of anything happening is in inverse proportion to its
desirability.   *Gumperson's Law*

The quality of moral behaviour varies in inverse proportion to the
number of human beings involved.   Aldous Huxley *Grey Eminence*

The probability of winning is inversely proportional to the amount of
the wager.   *McGoon's Law*

In every restaurant, the hardness of the butter increases in direct
proportion to the softness of the bread being served.
                                                   Harriet Markman (1991)

In political discussion, heat is in inverse proportion to knowledge.
                                                            J. G. Minchin

The speed of exit of a civil servant is in direct proportion to the
quality of his service.   Ralph Nader *The Spoiled System*

The length of a country's national anthem is inversely proportional to
the importance of that country.   Alan L. Otten

The time spent on any item of the agenda will be in inverse proportion to the sum involved.
                C. Northcote Parkinson *Parkinson's Law of Triviality* (1957)

The degree of one's emotion varies in inverse proportion with one's
knowledge of the facts – the less you know, the hotter you get.
                                                         Bertrand Russell

The length of a meeting rises in direct proportion with the square of
the number of people present, and awake.
                                        Eileen Shanahan *Shanahan's Law*

Appealingness is in inverse proportion to attainability.
                                            John Updike *New Yorker* (1975)

The probability of failure is directly proportional to the number and
importance of the people watching.   *Zumwelt's Law*

The angle of the dangle is inversely proportional to the heat of the
meat.   *Law of Male Sexual Excitement*

The probability of a piece of bread landing butter side down is
directly proportional to the cost of the carpet.   Anon

—————— **" PURE "** ——————

SHE WAS AS PURE AS THE DRIVEN SNOW. ANON

She was as pure as the driven snow – but she drifted.

H. W. Thompson *Body, Boots and Britches* (1940)

I am as pure as the driven slush. Talullah Bankhead

—————— **" PURSE "** ——————

YOU CAN'T MAKE A SILK PURSE OUT OF A SOW'S EAR. JONATHAN SWIFT *POLITE CONVERSATIONS* (1738)

You could cover the sow's ear with a silk purse, and the bristles would still work through. Marie Lloyd

You can't make a purse out of somebody's ear.

Clifford Odets *Golden Boy* (1937)

He has made a silk purse out of a sow's ear.

Hugh Pentecost *I'll Sing at your Funeral* (1942)

Those who devote themselves to making a silk purse out of a sow's ear are in duty bound to go the whole hog. Kenneth Tynan

You can't make a silk purse out of sow's ear, but you can make the most lovely homemade wine.

Merrily Harpur *The Nightmares of Dream Topping*

You can't make a silk purse out of a spoiled child. L. L. Levinson

—————— **" PURSUIT "** ——————

THE ENGLISH COUNTRY GENTLEMAN GALLOPING AFTER A FOX: THE UNSPEAKABLE IN FULL PURSUIT OF THE UNEATABLE.

OSCAR WILDE *A WOMAN OF NO IMPORTANCE* (1893)

Golf is the unthinkable in pursuit of the unsinkable. Douglas Watkinson

The synthetic indignation of certain English cricketers over alleged Pakistani ball-tampering: the unedifying in pursuit of the unbeatable. Patrick Collins *Mail on Sunday* (1992)

"PUT"

PUT THAT IN YOUR PIPE . . . AND SMOKE IT.

R. H. BARHAM *LAY OF ST ODILLE* (1840)

Put that on your needle and knit it.   Ngaio Marsh (1941)

I'LL PUT MY CART BEFORE THE HORSE, LIKE
HOMER.   CICERO (c. 50 BC)

On an eloping student – She put the heart before the course.

George S. Kaufman (1935)

Said Descartes, *I extol*
Myself because I have a soul
And beasts do not (Of course
He had to put Descartes before the horse.)

Clifton Fadiman *Theological (c. 1950)*

Always put Horace before Descartes.   Donald O. Rickter

He locked the stable door while they were putting the cart before the
   horse.   Stanley Walker *New Yorker* (1941)

" QUESTION "

TO BE OR NOT TO BE, THAT IS THE QUESTION:
WHETHER 'TIS NOBLER IN THE MIND TO SUFFER
THE SLINGS AND ARROWS OF OUTRAGEOUS
FORTUNE
OR TO TAKE ARMS AGAINST A SEA OF TROUBLES,
AND OPPOSING END THEM.

WILLIAM SHAKESPEARE *HAMLET* (1602)

To be, or not to be: that is the question:
Whether 'tis better in this life to suffer
The petty trials of unmarried life
Or add one more unto a list of troubles,
And thus by marriage end them?   William H. Edmunds *Weekly Dispatch* (1880)

To print, or not to print – that is the question.
Whether 'tis better in a trunk to bury
The quirks and crotchets of outrageous fancy.
Or send a well-wrote copy to the press,
And by disclosing, end them?   Richard Jago

Modern soliloquy: Well, frankly, the problem as I see it at this
    moment in time is whether I should just lie down under all this
    hassle and let them walk all over me, or whether I should say OK,
    I get the message, and do myself in.   Prince Charles (1989)

T.B. or not T.B., that is congestion.   Woody Allen

On croquet – To peg out or not to peg out – that is the question.
                                                        J. W. Solomon

On dramatic criticism – To boo or not to boo, that is the question.
                                          Michael Billington *The Guardian*

On political correctness – P.C. or not P.C., that was 1993s burning
    question.   *Sunday Times* (1993)

Toupee or not toupee, that is the question.   Anon

To pee or not to pee.   Anon

Tabby or not tabby, cat is the question.   Colin M. Jarman

—————— ❝ RACE ❞ ——————

THE RACE IS NOT TO THE SWIFT, NOR THE BATTLE
TO THE STRONG,   ECCLESIASTES 9:11 *THE BIBLE*

The race *is* to the swift, the battle *to* the strong.   John Davidson

The race is not always to the swift, nor the battle to the strong, but
    that's the way to bet.   Damon Runyon

The race was not to the swift after all, it was to the indefatigably
    inconsequential and life was random.   Tom Sharpe *Wilt* (1976)

—————— ❝ RAIDER ❞ ——————

RAIDERS OF THE LOST ARK.   *FILM TITLE* (1981)

On Ted Turner's colorization of old black and white movies – Raider of
    the lost archives.   *American Film* (1989)

On Shane Warne (Australian leg-spinner) – Raider of the lost art.
                                          Bob Holmes *Observer* (1994)

—————— ❝ REAL ❞ ——————

REAL MEN DON'T EAT QUICHE.
                                    BRUCE FEIRSTEIN *PLAYBOY* (1982)

Once 007 was licensed to kill, now he not only eats quiche, but he
    cooks it himself.   Chris Peachment *Time Out* (1985)

On George Bush's tennis style – Real men don't lob.   *Runners' World*

Real men don't carry umbrellas.   Jill Parkin *Daily Express* (1992)

Reel men do eat fish.   Anon

—————— 💥 REBEL 💥 ——————

REBEL WITHOUT A CAUSE.   *FILM TITLE* (1955)

Rebel without a chord.   Tom Petty *Song title*

On 'The Name of the Father' (1993) – Rebel film without an IRA
   cause.   Alexander Walker *Evening Standard*

On Che Guevara (Revolutionary) – Rebel without a pause.   Anon

On Ronald Reagan (US president) – A rebel without a clue.   Anon

—————— 💥 RECESSION 💥 ——————

RECESSION IS WHEN A NEIGHBOUR LOSES HIS JOB; DEPRESSION IS WHEN YOU LOSE YOURS.   ANON

Depression is when you are out of work. Recession is when a
   neighbour is out of work. A recovery is when Jimmy Carter is
   out of work.   Ronald Reagan

—————— 💥 REFUGE 💥 ——————

PATRIOTISM IS THE LAST REFUGE OF A SCOUNDREL.   SAMUEL JOHNSON

Work is the refuge of people who have nothing better to do. Oscar Wilde

Ambition is the last refuge of failure.   Oscar Wilde

Consistency is the last refuge of the unimaginative.   Oscar Wilde

Seriousness is the only refuge of the shallow.   Oscar Wilde

Crying is the last refuge of plain women, but the ruin of pretty ones.
   Oscar Wilde

Philanthropy is the refuge of people who wish to annoy their fellow
   creatures.   Oscar Wilde *An Ideal Husband* (1895)

Simple pleasures are the last refuge of the complex.   Oscar Wilde

Democracy, the last refuge of cheap misgovernment.   G. B. Shaw

In Dr. Johnson's famous dictionary patriotism is defined as the last refuge of a scoundrel. With all due respect to an enlightened but inferior lexicographer I beg to submit that it is the first.

Ambrose Bierce

Sex is the last refuge of the miserable.

Quentin Crisp *The Naked Civil Servant* (1968)

Patriotism is seen not only as the last refuge of the scoundrel but as the first bolt-hole of the hypocrite. Melvyn Bragg *Speak for England*

—— **❝ REPRESENTATION ❞** ——

TAXATION WITHOUT REPRESENTATION IS TYRANNY. JAMES OTIS (1761)

If James Otis thought taxation without representation was bad, he should see how bad it is *with* representation. *Old Farmer's Almanac*

On the lack of British influence in the United Nations – No annihilation without representation. Arnold Toynbee (1947)

Artificial insemination is copulation without representation. *Playboy*

—— **❝ RICH ❞** ——

I AM RICH BEYOND THE DREAMS OF AVARICE.
EDWARD MOORE *THE GAMESTER* (1753)

We're wealthy – not beyond the dreams of average. O. Henry (1908)

Bertie's father was rich beyond the dreams of actresses.
Edgar Wallace *The Mind of Mr J. G. Reeder* (1925)

LET ME TELL YOU ABOUT THE VERY RICH. THEY ARE DIFFERENT FROM YOU AND ME. F. SCOTT FITZGERALD

(*Ernest Hemingway replied* – Yes, they have more money)

The rich are different from you and me because they have more credit. John Leonard *New York Times*

THE MAN WHO DIES RICH, DIES DISGRACED.
ANDREW CARNEGIE (c. 1900)

The man who lives rich, lives disgraced. Aga Khan III

" RIGHT "

THE MINORITY IS ALWAYS RIGHT.

HENRIK IBSEN *AN ENEMY OF THE PEOPLE* (1882)

The customer is always right. H. G. Selfridge

The public is always right. Cecil B. de Mille

The public is never wrong. Adolph Zukor

Psychiatry is the only business where the customer is always wrong.

Anon

" ROOST "

CURSES ARE LIKE YOUNG CHICKENS – THEY ALWAYS COME HOME TO ROOST.

ROBERT SOUTHEY *THE CURSE OF KEHAMA* (1810)

Frank Bruno says I'm chicken. Well, you can tell him I've come home to roost. Joe Bugner

It's been a real gravy train for a long time now; now the gravy has come home to roost on the shirt. Robbie Vincent

On the Conservative government – The headless chickens have come home to roost. *Daily Mail* (1994)

" ROOT "

THE LOVE OF MONEY IS THE ROOT OF ALL EVIL.

TIMOTHY 6:10 *THE BIBLE*

Money is the fruit of evil, as often as the root of it. Henry Fielding

Industry is the root of all ugliness. Oscar Wilde

The lack of money is the root of all evil. G. B. Shaw *Man and Superman*

The love of economy is the root of all virtue. G. B. Shaw *Maxims* (1903)

Ignorance is the root of all evil. Ruth Feiner (1942)

The love of truth lies at the root of much humour. Robertson Davies

Money is the root of all good. Minnesota Fats

Money is the root of all evil . . . but that's one evil I'm rooting for.
W. L. Deandrea *Killed in Ratings* (1978)

Women are the root of all evil. American saying

Crime is the root of all evil. American saying

Money is the root of all evil, but avarice is the compost. Irish saying

We have come to the conclusion that it's not money but theories
about it that are the root of all evil. Anon

Money is the sauce of all evil. Anon

Monkey is the root of all evil. Graffiti

" ROPE "

GIVE THE THIEF ENOUGH ROPE AND HE'LL HANG HIMSELF. PROVERB

Give a man enough rope and he'll skip. Zsa Zsa Gabor

On Charles Haughey (Irish Prime Minister) – I have a theory about
Charles Haughey. Give him enough rope and he'll hang you.
Leo Enright (1992)

Give a girl enough rope and she'll ring the wedding bells. Anon

Give a quack enough rope and he'll hang up a shingle. Anon

" ROSE "

GATHER YE ROSEBUDS WHILE YE MAY,
OLD TIME IS STILL A-FLYING:
AND THIS SAME FLOWER THAT SMILES TO-DAY,
TO-MORROW WILL BE DYING.

ROBERT HERRICK *TO THE VIRGINS* (1648)

Gather ye rosebuds where ye may; florists are very expensive.
Kenneth Kahn

Gather ye bank-notes while ye may;
The happy time is flitting:
The Member canvassing today
Tomorrow will be sitting. Anon *Election Time*

MY LUVE'S LIKE A RED, RED ROSE.

ROBERT BURNS *MY LUVE IS LIKE A RED RED ROSE*

Suppose our word for rose had come from the Netherlands – angli-
cized as stinkbloom. What follows? My love is like a red, red
stinkbloom. Arthur Marshall

My loaf is like a weird, weird rose. Frank Muir *My Word* (1973)

My love's like a red, red nose. Anon

ROSE IS A ROSE IS A ROSE IS A ROSE.

GERTRUDE STEIN *SACRED EMILY*

Like the rose, mighty like the rose, a rose is a rose is an onion.

Ernest Hemingway *For Whom the Bell Tolls* (1940)

Piano is a piano is a piano – Gertrude Steinway.　　　　　　Graffiti

WHAT'S IN A NAME? THAT WHICH WE CALL A ROSE BY ANY OTHER NAME WOULD SMELL AS SWEET.

WILLIAM SHAKESPEARE *ROMEO & JULIET* (1595)

A cabbage by any other name would smell as sweet.

Clyde Fitch *Captain James* (1901)

A corpse by any other name . . .　　　R. A. Walling *Book title* (1943)

A rose by any other name would be just as expensive.　　Lambert Jeffries

A chrysanthemum by any other name would be easier to spell.

William J. Johnston *Reader's Digest*

A rose by any other name would show you're ignorance about
flowers.　　　　　　　　　　　　　　　　　　　　　Anon

———————— ❝ SAFE ❞ ————————

JUST WHEN YOU THOUGHT IT SAFE TO GO BACK IN THE WATER.　　MOVIE PUBLICITY SLOGAN FOR *JAWS 2* (1978)

Just when *he* thought it was safe to go back in the water.

Movie publicity slogan for *10* (1979)

On 'Alien' (1979) – Just when you thought it was safe to go back into
space.　　　　　　　　　　　　　　　　　　　　John Stanley

Just when you thought it was safe to go back into the departure
lounge.　　　　　　　Movie publicity slogan for *Airplane 2* (1980)

Now you're not safe out of the water.

Movie publicity slogan for *Piranha 2: The Flying Killers*

On 'Jaws 3-D' (1983) – Just when you thought it was safe to go back
into the cinema, a new *Jaws* hits the screens, this time in 3-D.

Derek Adams *Time Out*

Just when you thought it was safe to get back into a bikini.

Observer (1989)

Just when you thought it was safe to go back and drink the water.

Anon

Just when you thought it was safe to get back into bed.　　Anon

On 'Jaws 3-D' (1983) – Just when you thought it was safe to go back
to the toilet.　　　　　　　　　　　　　　　　　　Graffiti

—— **" SAID "** ——

LEAST SAID IS SOONEST MENDED. PROVERB

Least said is soonest amended.   Miguel de Cervantes *Don Quixote* (1615)

Least said is soonest disavowed.   Ambrose Bierce *The Devil's Dictionary* (1911)

Of Ian Botham's innings yesterday, soon said least mended, I think.
Jack Bannister – BBC TV Cricket commentary

—— **" SALT "** ——

YOU ARE THE SALT OF THE EARTH.

MATTHEW 5:13 *THE BIBLE*

Retired sea-captains, some of the salt of the earth, who had formerly been the salt of the sea.   Henry D. Thoreau *Cape Cod* (1855)

The point is that nobody likes to have salt rubbed in their wounds, even if it is the salt of the earth.   Rebecca West

I do not consider it a compliment to be called 'the salt of the earth'. Salt is used for some one else's food. It dissolves in that food. And salt is good only in small quantities. Chaim Weizmann *Trial and Error* (1949)

On Jimmy Walker (Mayor of New York) – In my estimation he is the cream of the earth.   Frank Hague

—— **" SAY "** ——

On making a speech in the House of Commons – **DON'T QUOTE LATIN; SAY WHAT YOU HAVE TO SAY, AND THEN SIT DOWN.** DUKE OF WELLINGTON

There are three golden rules for Parliamentary speakers: Stand up, speak up and shut up!   J. W. Lowther (1919)

On making a speech in the House of Commons – Say what you have to say and the first time you come to a sentence with a grammatical ending – sit down.   Sir Winston Churchill

On making a public speech – Stand up (to be seen), speak up (to be heard), shut up (to be applauded), sit down (to be appreciated).
Androyne Bezuidenhout

On making a public speech – Be sincere, be brief, be seated.   Anon

" SCRATCH "

SCRATCH THE RUSSIAN AND YOU WILL FIND THE TARTAR.
JOSEPH DE MAISTRE (c. 1815)

Scratch the Christian and you will find the pagan – spoiled.
Israel Zangwill *Children of the Ghetto* (1892)

Scratch a Puerto Rican and you will find a Spaniard underneath.
F. A. Ober *Puerto Rico* (1899)

Scratch an artist and you surprise a child.
James G. Huneker

Scratch an actor and you will find an actress.
Dorothy Parker

Scratch a writer and find a social climber.
Dorothy Parker

Scratch a pessimist, and you often find a defender of privilege.
Lord William Beveridge (1943)

Scratch a Pole and you find a Pole, even if he is a Communist.
J. Flanner *New Yorker* (1947)

Scratch an American and you get a Seventh Day Adventist every time.
Lord Hailsham (1969)

Every writer thinks he is capable of anything. Scratch a Faulkner or a
Hemingway and you'll find a man who thinks he can run the
world.
Norman Mailer *Nova* (1969)

Scratch a fanatic and you'll find a wound that never healed.
William N. Jayme *Newsweek* (1973)

Scratch most feminists and underneath there is a woman who longs to
be a sex object, the difference is that is not *all* she longs to be.
Betty Rollin *First, You Cry* (1976)

Scratch a marathon runner once and they tell you how wonderful they
feel. Scratch them twice and they tell you about their latest injuries.
Arnold Cooper (1981)

" SCUM "

On the British Army – **OURS IS COMPOSED OF THE SCUM
OF THE EARTH, THEY HAVE ENLISTED FOR DRINK,
THAT IS THE SIMPLE TRUTH.**
DUKE OF WELLINGTON (1831)

The rich are the scum of the earth in every country.
G. K. Chesterton *The Flying Inn*

A good rugby team is the scrum of the earth.
Anon

❝ SECRET ❞

THE ONLY SECRET A WOMAN CAN KEEP IS HER AGE.

PROVERB

The only secret a woman can keep is the one she doesn't know.

French Proverb

❝ SEE ❞

IS THIS A DAGGER WHICH I SEE BEFORE ME?

WILLIAM SHAKESPEARE *MACBETH* (1606)

Is this Heidegger which I see before me?

Colin M. Jarman

❝ SERVE ❞

NO MAN CAN SERVE TWO MASTERS . . . YOU CANNOT SERVE GOD AND MAMMON.

MATTHEW 6:24 *THE BIBLE*

Those who set out to serve both God and Mammon soon discover
that there is no God.
Logan Pearsall Smith *Afterthoughts* (1931)

On the choice of two fish courses – Thou canst serve both cod and
salmon.
Ada Beddington Leverson (1970)

THEY ALSO SERVE WHO ONLY STAND AND WAIT.

JOHN MILTON *SONNET: ON HIS BLINDNESS* (1655)

We also serve who only punctuate.

Brian Moore

❝ SHALT ❞

THOU SHALT NOT BEAR FALSE WITNESS AGAINST THY NEIGHBOUR.

EXODUS 20:16 *THE BIBLE*

There are 869 different forms of lying, but only one of them has been
squarely forbidden. Thou shalt not bear false witness against thy
neighbour.
Mark Twain (1893)

THOU SHALT NOT COMMIT ADULTERY.

EXODUS 20:14 *THE BIBLE*

Thou shalt not commit adultery . . . unless in the mood.
W. C. Fields

Do not adultery commit
Advantage rarely comes of it.
A. H. Clough *The Latest Decalogue*

THOU SHALT NOT COVET THY NEIGHBOUR'S HOUSE, THOU SHALT NOT COVET THY NEIGHBOUR'S WIFE.
EXODUS 20:17 *THE BIBLE*

Thou shalt not covet; but tradition
Approves all forms of competition.
A. H. Clough *The Latest Decalogue*

THOU SHALT NOT KILL.

Thou shalt not kill; but need'st not strive
 Officiously to keep alive.
A. H. Clough *The Latest Decalogue*

The idea of a Supreme Being who creates a world in which one
 creature is designed to eat another in order to subsist, and then
 pass a law saying, 'Thou shalt not kill,' is so monstrously. immeas-
 urably, bottomlessly absurd that I am at a loss to understand how
 mankind has entertained or given it house room all this long.
Peter de Vries

THOU SHALT NOT STEAL.
EXODUS 20:15 *THE BIBLE*

Do not steal; thou'lt never thus to compete
Successfully in business. Cheat.
Ambrose Bierce

Thou shalt not steal; an empty feat
When it's so lucrative to cheat.
A. H. Clough *The Latest Decalogue*

THOU SHALT ONLY HAVE ONE GOD.
EXODUS 20:1 *THE BIBLE*

Thou shalt have one God only; who
Would be at the expense of two?
A. H. Clough *The Latest Decalogue*

—————— **❝ SHEPHERD ❞** ——————

THE LORD IS A LOVING SHEPHERD.
THE BIBLE

The Lord is a shoving leopard.
Dr W. A. Spooner

WHILE SHEPHERDS WATCHED THEIR FLOCKS BY NIGHT.
NAHUM TATE (1700)

While shepherds washed their socks by night.
Anon

—————— **❝ SHOE ❞** ——————

IF THE SHOE FITS, WEAR IT.
SAYING

If the shoe fits, ask for it in another colour.
Beryl Pfizer

Have you ever noticed that when the shoe fits, it's not in the sale.
Angie Papadakis

❝ SHORT ❞

A FEW PECKS SHORT OF A BUSHEL.
ANON

On composer Erik Satie – A couple of instruments short of the full
orchestra, old Erik.
Martin James *Sunday Times* (1992)

On singer Sinead O'Connor – The sweet-voiced spamhead – talk about
one track short of a compilation album.
Time Out (1992)

On Prince Charles – A few gentleman's relish sandwiches short of a
shooting picnic.
Polly Toynbee *Radio Times* (1994)

A can short of a six-pack.
American saying

A few inches short of a pop-up toaster.
Anon

A few bricks short of a load.
Anon

❝ SHOW ME . . . ❞

SHOW ME A LIAR AND I WILL SHOW YOU A THIEF.
LATIN PROVERB

Show me a thoroughly satisfied man – and I will show you a failure.
Thomas A. Edison

Show me a poet and I'll show you a shit.
A. J. Liebling

Show me a critic without prejudices, and I'll show you an arrested
cretin.
George J. Nathan

Show me a hero and I'll write you a tragedy.
F. Scott Fitzgerald

Show me a great actor and I'll show you a lousy husband. Show me a
great actress and you've seen the devil.
W. C. Fields

Show me a good loser and I'll show you a man who is playing golf
with his boss.
Nebraska Fire-Eater

Show me a guy who's afraid to look bad and I'll show you a guy you
can beat every time.
Lou Brock

Show me a man with both feet firmly planted on the ground and I'll
show you a man making a crucial putt on the 18th green.
Herm Albright

Show me a college dean whose professors are out on strike and I'll show you someone who's no longer in possession of his faculties.
Bert Murray

Show me a man who has enjoyed his schooldays and I will show you a bully and a bore.
Robert Morley

Show me someone who never gossips and I'll show you someone who isn't interested in people.
Barbara Walters

Show me a congenital eavesdropper with the instincts of a Peeping Tom and I will show you the makings of a dramatist.
Kenneth Tynan

Show me a man who jogs every morning and I'll show you a breaking marriage.
Kenneth Robinson

Show me a man wearing matching hankerchief, socks and tie and I'll show you a man wearing a Xmas present.
Frank Case

Show me a nation whose national beverage is beer, and I'll show you an advanced toilet technology.
Paul Hawkins (1977)

Show me an orchestra that likes its conductor and I'll show you a lousy conductor.
Goddard Lieberson

Show me a butler with false teeth and I'll show you an indentured servant.
Arnold Harris

Show me a genuine case of platonic friendship, and I shall show you two old or homely faces.
Austin O'Malley

Show me a boring party and I'll show you a fête worse than death.
Kay Haugaard

Show me a talented football player who is thick and I'll show you a player who has problems.
Brian Clough

—————— "SIDES" ——————

THERE ARE TWO SIDES TO EVERY QUESTION.
PROTAGORAS (435 BC)

The man who sees both sides of a question is a man who sees absolutely nothing at all.
Oscar Wilde The Critic as Artist (1891)

There were two sides to every argument – his and the wrong side.
M. S. Michel The X-Ray Murder (1942)

There are four sides to every story: your side, my side, the right side and the United Nations' side.
Gerald Segal (1988)

The Pentagon has five sides on every issue.
Anon Russian politician

There are three sides to every question: your side, his side, and to hell with it.
Anon

There are two sides to every question that we're not interested in. Anon

There are two sides to every question and if you want to be popular you take both.   Anon

There are two sides to every question, and a politician usually takes both.   Anon

There are two sides to every question, except when it happens to be a love triangle.   Anon

There are two sides to every peace conference, but never an end.   Anon

There are three rides to every equestrian.   Colin M. Jarman

ᶜᶜ SIGH ᵗᵗ

SIGH NO MORE, LADIES SIGH NO MORE,
MEN WERE DECEIVERS EVER;
ONE FOOT IN SEA, AND ONE IN SHORE,
TO ONE THING CONSTANT NEVER.
THEN SIGH NOT SO,
BUT LET THEM GO,
AND BE YOU BLITHE AND BONNY,
CONVERTING ALL YOU SOUNDS OF WOE
INTO HEY NONNY, NONNY.

WILLIAM SHAKESPEARE *MUCH ADO ABOUT NOTHING* (1599)

Sigh no more, dealer, sigh no more,
Shares were unstable ever,
They often have been down before,
At high rates constant never.
Then sigh not so,
Soon up they'll go,
And you be blithe and funny,
Converting all your notes of woe
Into hey money, money.   Anon *Much Ado in the City*

ᶜᶜ SILENCE ᵗᵗ

IF SPEECH IS SILVERN, THEN SILENCE IS GOLDEN.

MIDRASH LEVITICUS RABBAH (600)

Speech is great, but silence is greater.   Thomas Carlyle

Speech is fractional, silence is integral.   Henry D. Thoreau (1840)

Silence is not always tact, and it is tact, that is golden, not silence.
         Samuel Butler *Note Books* (1912)

Silence is golden, but sometimes invisibility is golder.   Ogden Nash (1938)

Silence is not golden, it's yellow.   Tom Anderson (1975)

The fact that silence is golden may explain why there is so little of it.
         Anon

Silence is not always golden – sometimes it is guilt.   Anon

Speech is silver, silence is golden and oratory is mainly brass.   Anon

❝ SINCEREST ❞

IMITATION IS THE SINCEREST FORM OF FLATTERY.
CHARLES C. COLTON *LACON* (1820)

Envy is the sincerest form of flattery.   Churlton Collins (1904)

Imitation is the sincerest form of television.   Fred Allen

Immigration is the sincerest form of flattery.   *Life*

Imitation is certainly the sincerest form of political desperation.
         Harold Wilson

Imitation is the sincerest form of TV ratings success.
         Alan Frank *The Science Fiction Handbook* (1982)

Ingratiation is the sincerest form of flattery.   Anon

Arms limitation is the sincerest form of flattery.   Anon

❝ SINS ❞

THE SEVEN DEADLY SINS: PRIDE, ENVY, SLOTH, GLUTTONY, AVARICE, IRE AND LUST.
GEOFFREY CHAUCER (1386)

The seven deadly sins: Food, clothing, firing, rent, taxes, respectability
and children.   G. B. Shaw *Major Barbara* (1905)

The seven deadly whims: New lips to kiss, Freedom from convention,
A new world for women, No more chaperons, Life with a kick in
it, The single moral standard, and Our own latchkey.
         Gloria Swanson *Prodigal Daughters* (1923)

" SKELETON "

THEY HAVE A SKELETON IN THEIR CLOSETS, AS WELL AS THEIR NEIGHBOURS.

WILLIAM M. THACKERAY *THE NEWCOMES* (1855)

His skeleton came out the cupboard, and gibbered at him.

F. Anstey *The Giant's Robe* (1884)

Not only is there a skeleton in every cupboard, but there is a screw loose in every skeleton. Samuel Butler

I would never run for President. Some people have skeletons in their closets, but I have a graveyard. Sylvester Stallone

" SLAVES "

RULE, BRITANNIA, RULE THE WAVES; BRITONS NEVER WILL BE SLAVES.

JAMES THOMSON *ALFRED: A MASQUE* (1740)

Englishmen will never be slaves; they are free to do whatever the Government and public opinion allow them to do. G. B. Shaw

He gives thanks that Britons will never be Slavs. Philip Guedella

" SLICE "

NO MATTER HOW YOU SLICE IT, IT'S STILL BALONEY.
ALFRED E. SMITH *SPEECH* (1936)

Slice him where you like, a hellhound is always a hellhound.

P. G. Wodehouse

Much of what Henry Wallace calls his global thinking is, no matter how you slice it, still *Globaloney*. Clare Booth Luce (1943)

" SMOKE "

THERE IS NO SMOKE WITHOUT FIRE.

FRENCH PROVERB (c. 1200)

There's no smoke without taxes. R. Linshaw

When there's smoke, there's toast.   J. C. Thomas
There's no smoke without mud being flung around.   Edwina Currie
Where there's smoke, there must be someone smoking.
                                            Movie publicity slogan for *Easy Living* (1937)

—— ❝ SOFT ❞ ——

A SOFT ANSWER TURNETH AWAY WRATH.

PROVERBS 15:1 *THE BIBLE*

A soft drink turneth away company.   Oliver Herford

—— ❝ SOFTLY ❞ ——

SPEAK SOFTLY, AND CARRY A BIG STICK.

THEODORE ROOSEVELT *SPEECH* (1901)

Speak softly, and carry a big carrot.   Howard C. Lauer
Clint Eastwood is a man who walks softly and carries a big percentage
   of the gross.   Bob Hope
Walk softly and carry an armoured tank division.   *A Few Good Men* (1992)
Speak softly and carry a big wallet.   Anon

—— ❝ SOLD ❞ ——

ESAU SOLD HIS BIRTHRIGHT FOR A MESS OF
POTAGE.

GENEVA BIBLE (Heading to Genesis 25)

Esau that swapped his copyright for a partridge.   O. Henry *Cupid à la Carte*
H. G. Wells sold his birthright for a pot of message.   Anon

—— ❝ SOLDIERS ❞ ——

OLD SOLDIERS NEVER DIE.   J. FOLEY *SONG TITLE* (1920)

Old soldiers never die, they simply fade away.
                        Brophy and Partridge *Songs of the British Soldiers* (1930)

There is an old saying that old soldiers never die – but they may starve, when other State pensioners are receiving increased benefits.
The Times (1940)

Union leaders have complained to the Government that old soldiers never die, but are given jobs in the Civil Service. *Daily Telegraph* (1979)

Old soldiers never die, they just write their memoirs. Art Buchwald

Old soldiers, she knew, never died; in her father's case it was not so much that he was fading away as he'd never been there in the first place. Beryl Bainbridge *Sweet William*

Old soldiers never die, only young ones. Anon

Old soldiers never die, just their privates. Graffiti

Old soldiers never die, they just get their deserts. Colin M. Jarman

—— **" SORROW "** ——

PARTING IS SUCH SWEET SORROW.

WILLIAM SHAKESPEARE *ROMEO AND JULIET* (1596)

Partying is such sweet sorrow. Robert Byrne

—— **" SORRY "** ——

LOVE MEANS NEVER HAVING TO SAY YOU'RE SORRY.

ERICH SEGAL *LOVE STORY* (1970)

Vasectomy means never having to say you're sorry. Larry Adler

Love means never having to say you're ugly.
Publicity slogan for *The Abominable Dr. Phibes* (1971)

Richard Nixon means never having to say you're sorry. Wilfrid Sheed

In the long view of film history only talent means never having to say you are sorry. Richard Corliss

Being Hindu means never having to say you're sorry.
Gita Mehta *Karma Cola* (1980)

Love means never having to say you're pregnant. Anon

After the shooting down of a Korean airliner – Being Russian means never having to say you're sorry. American Graffiti (1983)

Necrophilia means never having to say you're sorry. Graffiti

Constipation means never having to give a shit. Graffiti

❝ SOUL ❞

BREVITY IS THE SOUL OF WIT.

WILLIAM SHAKEPEARE *HAMLET* (1602)

Brevity is the soul of drinking.   Charles Lamb

Impropriety is the soul of wit.

W. Somerset Maugham *The Moon and the Sixpence*

Brevity is the soul of lingerie, as the Petticoat said to the Chemise.

Dorothy Parker

Logic is the soul of wit, not wisdom, that's why wit is funny.

Lincoln Steffens

Levity is the soul of wit.   Melville D. Landon

Brevity may be the soul of wit, but not when someone is saying I
   Love you!   Judith Viorst *Redbook* (1975)

❝ SOUND ❞

THE HILLS ARE ALIVE WITH THE SOUND OF MUSIC.

OSCAR HAMMERSTEIN II *SONG TITLE* (1959)

On 'Mistress of Novices' (1973) – The hills are alive with the sound of
   clichés.   Sheridan Morley

❝ SPACE ❞

IN SPACE NO ONE CAN HEAR YOU SCREAM.

MOVIE PUBLICITY SLOGAN FOR *ALIEN* (1979)

In space, no one can hear you laugh.   Miles Kington

On 'Alien 3' (1992) – In space no one can hear you yawn!   Sue Heal

❝ SPADE ❞

THE WISE MAN WILL CALL A SPADE A SPADE.

CICERO (46 BC)

Chesham does not like to call a spade a spade. He calls it a
   horticultural utensil.   William M. Thackeray *Philip* (1862)

The man who could call a spade a spade should be compelled to use
one. It is the only thing he is fit for.
Oscar Wilde

A lisp is when you call a spade a thpade.
Oliver Herford

If you call a spade a spade, you won't last long in advertising.
Anon

❝ SPEAK ❞

SPEAK NO EVIL OF THE DEAD. SOLON (c. 600 BC)

The maxim of not speaking evil of the dead should be reversed. We
should speak evil only of the dead, for in so doing we can do them
no harm.
Benjamin Franklin

Since we have to speak well of the dead, let's knock them while
they're still alive.
John Sloan

THINK TWICE, THEN SPEAK. PROVERB

Think twice before you speak and say it to yourself.
Elbert Hubbard *Philistine* (1902)

Think before you speak is criticism's motto; Speak before you think is
creation's.
E. M. Forster *Two Cheers for Democracy*

The wise man thinks once before he speaks twice.
Robert Benchley

Think twice before you speak – and you'll find everyone talking about
something else.
Francis Rodman

If you think before you speak, the other fellow gets his joke in first.
Ed Howe

Think before you think.
Stanislaw Lec

❝ SPOIL ❞

TOO MANY COOKS SPOIL THE BROTH.
BALTHAZAR GERBER *DISCOURSE OF BUILDING* (1662)

A common weakness with writers is to over-multiply the mysteries.
Too many crooks spoil the broth.
Ivor Brown

Too many crooks spoil the percentage.
H. Chandler

On 'La Cage aux Folles III' (1985) – Lots of cooks but not much
broth.
Variety

Too many cooks spoil the brothel.
Polly Adler

Too many kirks spoil Arbroath.
Frank Muir *My Word* (1980)

" SPREAD "

MONEY IS LIKE MANURE, NOT GOOD EXCEPT IT BE SPREAD AROUND.
FRANCIS BACON *ESSAYS* (1625)

Gossip and manure are only good for one thing – and that's
spreading. Gossip don't mean a damn unless you spread it around.
Doris Lilley

Culture is like jam. The less you have the more you spread it around.
French Graffiti (1968)

" STAGE "

ALL THE WORLD'S A STAGE, AND ALL THE MEN AND WOMEN MERELY PLAYERS.
WILLIAM SHAKESPEARE *AS YOU LIKE IT* (1599)

All the world is a stage, but the play is badly cast.   Oscar Wilde

All the world's a stage: we act but can't rehearse.
David McCord *Ultimate Necessity* (1941)

All the world's a stage, and most of us are desperately
under-rehearsed.   Sean O'Casey

If all the world's a stage, and all the men and women merely players,
where do the audiences come from?   Denis Nordern

The world is a stage, but most of us are stagehands.   Anon

" STAND "

DON'T JUST STAND THERE, DO SOMETHING.
ANON SAYING

To Gipsy Rose Lee – Don't just stand there, undo something.
Bob Hope (1940s)

Don't just do something, stand there!   Father Philip Bonigan

Don't just lie there, say something.   *Film title* (1973)

To an over-active actor – Don't do anything, just stand there.   Anon

❝ STATESMAN ❞

A STATESMAN IS A SUCCESSFUL POLITICIAN WHO IS DEAD. THOMAS REED

A statesman is a politician who's dead and now I know what a statesman is – we need more statesmen. Bob Edwards

❝ STONE ❞

HE THAT IS WITHOUT SIN AMONG YOU, LET HIM FIRST CAST A STONE AT HER. JOHN *THE BIBLE*

Alexander Woollcott always praises the first production of each season, being reluctant to stone the first cast. Walter Winchell

Let he who was never stoned cast the first sin. Howie Schneider

LEAVE NO STONE UNTURNED. PROVERB

A critic is a man who leaves no turn unstoned. G. B. Shaw

I am a conscientious man, when I throw rocks at seabirds I leave no tern unstoned. Ogden Nash

A ROLLING STONE GATHERS NO MOSS. ERASMUS (c. 1500)

Too much improvisation leaves the mind stupidly void. Running beer gathers no foam. Victor Hugo *Les Miserables* (1862)

We keep repeating the silly proverb that rolling stones gather no moss, as if moss were a desirable parasite. G. B. Shaw

A rolling stone gathers no moss, but a tethered sheep winna get fat. F. C. Bridge (1917)

On the feminist Lucy Stone League – A Lucy Stone gathers no boss. George S. Kaufman

If you do your rolling up hill you will gather some moss. *Meditations in Wall Street* (1940)

A rolling stone gathers no moss, but it gains a certain polish. Oliver Herford

I suppose it is quite necessary for them to be turning every stone to take the moss off. Theodora DuBois *Wild Duck Murders* (1943)

❝ STOPS ❞

THE BUCK STOPS HERE. HARRY S TRUMAN (c. 1945)

The buck stops with the guy who signs the cheques. Rupert Murdoch

The puck stops here.   Ice Hockey Saying
On Richard Nixon's Memoirs – The book stops here.   Anon (1978)
On President Bill Clinton – The f*** stops here.   *Private Eye* (1994)
The bus stops here . . . sometimes.   London Transport Graffiti

❝ STORM ❞

A STORM IN A TEA-CUP.   W. B. BERNARD *PLAY TITLE*
It was a storm in a tea-cup, but we politicians sail in paper boats.
                                                            Harold Macmillan
And so before a storm in a tea-cup brews, nip it in the bud.
                                                            Russell Grant

❝ STRAW ❞

IT IS THE LAST STRAW THAT BREAKS THE CAMEL'S
BACK.   ARCHBISHOP JOHN BRAMHALL *WORKS* (1655)
The last straw breaks the camel's back, but at least a large proportion
of the other straws serve to develop its muscles. Van Wyck Brooks (1942)

❝ STRIKE ❞

STRIKE WHILE THE IRON IS HOT.   FRENCH PROVERB (c. 1200)
Strike while the irony is hot.   Don Quinn

❝ SUCCEED ❞

IF AT FIRST YOU DON'T SUCCEED, TRY, TRY, AGAIN.
                                                    ROBERT THE BRUCE Attrib.
If at first you don't succeed, try, try, again. Then quit. There's no use
being a damn fool about it.   W. C. Fields
If at first you don't succeed, pry, pry, pry, again.
                                    Philip MacDonald *Warrant for X* (1937)

If at first you don't succeed, don't take any more chances.   Kin Hubbard

If at first you don't succeed, quit, quit, at once.   Stephen Leacock

If at first you don't succeed, you're doing about average.   L. L. Levinson

If at first you don't succeed, you're fired.   Jean Graman

If at first you don't suck seed, trier drier grain.   Frank Muir *My Word* (1974)

The simple secret of *Lucky Lady*'s plot is that if at first you don't
 ménage à trois, trois again.   Charles Champlin (1975)

If at first you don't succeed, you may not be encouraged to try again.
   Edwin McDowell *New York Times* (1988)

If at first you don't succeed, crawl into a hole, and cry, cry, again.
   E-Street – Sky TV (1993)

If you don't succeed at first, try second.   Baseball saying

If at first you don't succeed, try something else.   Anon

If at first you don't succeed, so much for sky diving.   Anon

If at first you don't succeed, try a little ardour.   Anon

If at first you don't succeed, try trying.   Anon

If at first you don't succeed, try, try again – to get someone to do it
 for you.   Anon

If at first you don't succeed, try, try to work out what it is you are
 doing wrong.   Anon

If at first you don't succeed, try looking in the waste-paper basket for
 instructions.   Anon

If at first you don't succeed, try doing it the way your wife first
 suggested.   Anon

If at first you don't succeed, *cheat*!   Graffiti

NOTHING SUCCEEDS LIKE SUCCESS.   FRENCH PROVERB

Moderation is a fatal thing . . . Nothing succeeds like excess.
   Oscar Wilde *A Woman of No Importance* (1893)

Nothing succeeds like failure.   Oliver Herford

Nothing succeeds, they say, like success. And certainly nothing fails
 like failure.   Margaret Drabble

Nothing succeeds like one's own successor.   Clarence H. Hincks

Nothing succeeds like reputation.   John Huston

Nothing recedes like success.   Walter Winchell

Nothing succeeds like success, except the failure that reverses it.
   Leo Stein *Journey into the Self*

Nothing succeeds like address.   Fran Lebowitz *Metropolitan Life* (1978)

Nothing succeeds like the appearance of success.
   Christopher Lasch *The Culture of Narcissism* (1979)

" SUMMER "

COME TO ARIZONA, WHERE SUMMER SPENDS THE WINTER.
ARIZONA TOURIST BOARD (1935)

Come to Arizona, where summer spends the winter . . . And Hell
  Spends the Summer.
Graffiti

ONE SWALLOW DOES NOT MAKE SUMMER.
AESOP *FABLES* (570 BC)

One fly makes a summer.
Mark Twain (1893)

One swallow does not make a summer, nor one goose a farmyard.
C. F. Rogers *Verify your References* (1938)

One swallow doesn't make a summer, but too many swallows make a
  fall.
George D. Prentice

One swallow doesn't make a summer, but one lark may make a fall.
Anon

SHALL I COMPARE THEE TO A SUMMER'S DAY?
THOU ART MORE LOVELY AND MORE TEMPERATE.
ROUGH WINDS DO SHAKE THE DARLING BUDS OF
MAY,
AND SUMMER'S LEASE HATH ALL TOO SHORT A
DATE
WILLIAM SHAKESPEARE *SONNETS*

Shall I equate thee with a summer's day?
Thou art more valid and more meaningful:
A north-west airstream will devalue May,
And summer's mortgage is forclosable.
Peter Titheradge

SUMMER IS ICUMEN IN,
LHUDE SING CUCCU!
GROWETH SED, AND BLOWETH MED,
AND SPRINGTH THE WUDE NU.
ANON *CUCKOO SONG* (c. 1250)

Winter is icumen in,
Lhude sing Goddamm.
Raineth drop and staineth slop,
And the world doth ramm!
Ezra Pound *Ancient Music*

Plumber is icumen in;
Bludie big tu-du.
Blowethe lampe, and showeth dampe,
And dripth the wud thru.
Bludie hel, boo-hoo!
A. Y. Campbell *Murie Sing*

" SUN "

MAKE HAY WHILE THE SUN SHINES.

JOHN HEYWOOD *DIALOGUE OF PROVERBS* (1565)

The Japanese policy is to make hell while the sun shines.

Sir Winston Churchill

THE SUN DOES NOT SET ON MY DOMINIONS.

PHILIP II OF SPAIN

His Majesty's dominions, on which the sun never sets.

Christopher North *Noctes Ambrosianae*

The sun never sets on the British Empire, because God wouldn't trust an Englishman in the dark. Duncan Sheath

THERE IS NOTHING NEW UNDER THE SUN.

ECCLESIASTES *THE BIBLE*

There is nothing new in the *Sun.* Jasper Carrott

" SUPPORT "

AN ATHEIST IS A MAN WHO HAS NO INVISIBLE MEANS OF SUPPORT. JOHN BUCHAN

A prejudice is a vagrant opinion without visible means of support.

Ambrose Bierce

SUPPORT THE RIGHT TO BEAR ARMS.

US NATIONAL RIFLE ASSOCIATION SLOGAN

Support the right to arm bears. American bumper sticker

" SURVIVAL "

His interpretation of Darwin's 'Theory of Evolution' – **THIS SURVIVAL OF THE FITTEST IMPLIES MULTIPLICATION OF THE FITTEST.**

HERBERT SPENCER *PRINCIPLES OF BIOLOGY* (1865)

Journalism justifies its own existence by the great Darwinian principle of the survival of the vulgarest. Oscar Wilde (1891)

The American language is in a state of flux based upon the survival of the unfittest.   Cyril Connolly

On the re-opening of the London City Ballet – Revival of the fittest.
           David Dougill *Sunday Times* (1993)

Capitalism is the survival of the fattest.   Graffiti

❝ SWEET ❞

SWEETS TO THE SWEET   WILLIAM SHAKESPEARE *HAMLET* (1602)

Sweets to the sweet have made much business for dentists.   Anon

❝ SWING ❞

IT DON'T MEAN A THING IF IT AIN'T GOT THAT SWING.   'DUKE' ELLINGTON AND IRVING MILLS *SONG TITLE* (1932)

A playground don't mean a thing if it ain't got a swing.
           Adrian Love – Jazz FM (1992)

❝ TAILORS ❞

IT TAKES NINE TAILORS TO MAKE A MAN.   PROVERB

It is a more common than convenient saying, that nine tailors make a man; it were well if nineteen could make a woman her mind.
         Nathaniel Ward *The Simple Cobbler* (1647)

They say it takes nine tailors to make a man – apparently, one is sufficient to ruin him.   Sir Walter Scott *Letter* (1819)

❝ TAKE ❞

YOU CAN'T TAKE IT WITH YOU WHEN YOU GO.
                 PROVERB

He couldn't take his money with him, for gold melts at a certain temperature.   Edgar Wallace *The Mind of Mr J. G. Reeder* (1925)

True, you can't take it with you, but then, that's not the place where it comes in handy. Brendan Francis

If I can't take it with me, I don't want to go. Mick Easterby

You can't take it with you when you go, where would you put it all? Steven Wright

You can't take it with you, but that's not the worst. The frustrating thing is most of it goes first. Anon

—— **❝ TALK ❞** ——

TALK IS CHEAP. PROVERB

Talk is cheap, but you can't buy it back. William Blatt

Talk is cheap, because supply exceeds demand. Anon

Talk is cheap, except at peak phone rates. Anon

Talk is cheap, which is why silence is golden. Colin M. Jarman

—— **❝ TEACH ❞** ——

YOU CANNOT TEACH AN OLD DOG NEW TRICKS.
WILLIAM CAMDEN *REMAINES* (1605)

You can't teach an old dogma new tricks. Dorothy Parker

You can't teach the old maestro a new tune.
Jack Kerouac *On the Road* (1957)

—— **❝ TEACHER ❞** ——

EXPERIENCE IS THE BEST TEACHER. LATIN PROVERB

Time is a great teacher, but unfortunately it kills all its pupils.
Hector Berlioz

Life is the best teacher of all, though the fees on occasion come somewhat expensive. Richard Gordon

Experience is a hard teacher because she gives the test first, the lessons afterwards. Vernon Law (1960)

" THIEF "

PROCRASTINATION IS THE THIEF OF TIME.

EDWARD YOUNG *NIGHT THOUGHTS* (1742)

Procrastination – not only thief but murderer of time.

M. Warren *Warren-Gerry Correspondence* (1787)

He was always late on principle, his principle being that punctuality is the thief of time.   Oscar Wilde *The Picture of Dorian Gray* (1891)

Opportunity is the thief of time.   James Huneker

Procrastination is all of the time.   Ogden Nash (1939)

Far from being the thief of time, procrastination is the king of it.

Ogden Nash *Primrose Path* (1940)

What once could leisurely be dwelt on . . . must go by the board, speed being the thief of time in our neck of the country.

P. van Greenaway *Dissident* (1980)

Procrastination is the thief of time; so are a lot of other long words.

Anon

Procreation is the thief of time.   Anon

Constipation is the thief of time.   Graffiti

" THINK "

I THINK THEREFORE I AM (*COGITO ERGO SUM*).

RENÉ DESCARTES *PRINCIPLES OF PHILOSOPHY* (1637)

I said, with the foolish philospher, I think, therefore I am. It was Woman who taught me to say, I am; therefore I think.

G. B. Shaw *Man and Superman* (1903)

The dictum might be improved, thus; *Cogito ergo cogito ergo sum* – I think that I think, therefore I think that I am.

Ambrose Bierce *The Devil's Dictionary* (1906)

Sometimes I think and sometimes I am.   Paul Valéry

I think, therefore I am – I think.   Howard Schneider

I think, therefore Descartes is.   Saul Steinberg

I bomb, therefore I am.   Philip Slater

Cogito ergo boom.   Susan Sontag *Styles of Radical Will* (1969)

Sexual freedom has become more important than identity. Indeed, it has superseded it. The modern philosophy states, I ejaculate, therefore I am.
Quentin Crisp

I think they're for 1 a.m.
Denis Nordern *My Word* (1978)

Rene Descartes was a drunken fart – I drink, therefore I am.
Monty Python's Flying Circus – BBC TV

I think, therefore I ambient.
Mixmaster Morris (1993)

I think therefore I.B.M.
I.B.M. Advertising slogan

Cogito ergo sum: I think, therefore I exist:
Coito ergo sum. I screw, therefore I sexist.
Anon

Edo ergo sum – I eat therefore I am.
Anon

I'm pink therefore I'm spam.
Anon

Cogito ergo spud – I think, therefore I yam.
Graffiti

I think, I think; therefore I think.
Graffiti

I am, therefore I think. (Is this putting Descartes before the Horse?)
Graffiti

" THINKING "

JOAN BAKEWELL – THE THINKING MAN'S PIECE OF CRUMPET.
FRANK MUIR

Since her name is Bakewell, she should have been called 'The thinking man's tart'.
Jo Brand *The Brain Drain* – BBC TV (1993)

I am actually called the thinking man's muffin.
Jo Brand *Ibid*

Jonathan Ross – The sinking man's David Letterman.
Garry Bushell *Modern Review* (1992)

Oliver Reed – The drinking man's thespian.
Anon

" TIGER "

TIGER! TIGER! BURNING BRIGHT
IN THE FORESTS OF THE NIGHT.
WILLIAM BLAKE *SONGS OF EXPERIENCE* (1794)

Tiger, tiger, my mistake;
I thought that you were William Blake.
Ogden Nash *Versus*

THREE – I

Inanimate objects are classified scientifically into three major categories: those that don't work, those that break down, and those that get lost. Russell Baker *New York Times* (1968)

I have three phobias which, could I mute them, would make my life as slick as a sonnet, but as dull as ditch water: I hate to go to bed, I hate to get up, and I hate to be alone. Tallulah Bankhead

Three things cost dear: the caresses of a dog, the love of a mistress, and the invasion of a host. H. G. Bohn *Handbook of Proverbs* (1855)

There are three ways to get something done: do it yourself, hire someone, or forbid your children to do it. Monta Crane

There are only three things to be done with a woman. You can love her, you can suffer her, or you can turn her into literature.
Lawrence Durrell *Justine* (1957)

There are three things not worth running for: a bus, a woman or a new economic panacea; if you wait a bit another one will come along. Derrick Heathcote-Amory

The three questions of greatest concern are: 1. Is it attractive? 2. Is it amusing? 3. Does it know its place? Fran Lebowitz *Metropolitan Life* (1978)

Three things sum up Welsh women: they are frugal in the market, they're pious in chapel, and they're rampant in bed. Ruth Madoc

Only three things are done in a hurry: flying from the plague, escaping quarrels, and catching fleas. *Philadelphia Port Folio* (1810)

There are three kinds of intelligence: the intelligence of man, the intelligence of the animals, and the intelligence of the military – in that order. Gottfried Reinhardt

There are three rules for writing the novel. Unfortunately, no one knows what they are. W. Somerset Maugham

There's three things you can do in a baseball game: you can win, you can lose, or it can rain. Casey Stengell

Three things are bad when lean: a goose, a goat, and a woman.
Portuguese proverb

Three things that are useless: whispering to the deaf, grieving for the dead, and advising a woman against her will. Welsh proverb

There are three things you can't hide: love, smoke and a man riding a camel. Anon

The three most useless things in the world: the Pope's testicles, a nun's breasts and a vote of thanks. Anon

" TIME "

NO TIME LIKE THE PRESENT.

MRS MANLEY *THE LOST LOVER* (1696)

There is no time like the pleasant. Oliver Herford

No present like the time. Sekonda watch advert (1993)

A STITCH IN TIME SAVES NINE.

PROVERB

A switch in time saves crime. Roy B. Newell

A lie in time saves nine. Addison Mizner

A woman on time is one in nine. Addison Mizner

A stitch in time saves embarrassment. L. L. Levinson

A stitch in time would have confused Einstein. Anon

'THE TIME HAS COME,' THE WALRUS SAID, 'TO TALK OF MANY THINGS: OF SHOES – AND SHIPS – AND SEALING WAX – OF CABBAGES – AND KINGS.'

LEWIS CARROLL *THROUGH THE LOOKING-GLASS* (1871)

'The time has come', the Walrus said, 'to talk of football pools,
   Of fixture lists and copyright, of clever men and fools.' Percy Rudd

TIME HEALS ALL WOUNDS.

PROVERB

Time wounds all heels. Jane Ace

TIME IS A GREAT HEALER.

GEOFFREY CHAUCER *TROILUS AND CRISEYDE* (1380)

Time is the best healer, when it isn't a killer. D. H. Lawrence *Letter* (1930)

Time is a great healer, but it's no beauty specialist. Anon

THE TIME IS OUT OF JOINT; O CURSED SPITE, THAT EVER I WAS BORN TO SET IT RIGHT.

WILLIAM SHAKESPEARE *HAMLET* (1602)

The times are out of joint; O cursed spite,
One place your watch is wrong; another right. Anon

A WEEK IS A LONG TIME IN POLITICS.

HAROLD WILSON *REMARK* (1965)

A week is a long time in politics, and three weeks is twice as long.
Rosie Barnes

2,400 seconds is a long time in television. *Independent* (1989)

— **"TODAY AND TOMORROW"** —

DON'T PUT OFF TILL TOMORROW WHAT CAN BE DONE TODAY.   PROVERB

Never do today what you can put off till tomorrow.
C. H. Spurgeon *John Ploughman's Talk* (1869)

Don't put off till tomorrow what can be enjoyed today.   Josh Billings

It is well to put off till tomorrow what you ought not to do at all. Anon

Procrastination is putting off until tomorrow what you put off
yesterday until today.   Anon

Don't put off till tomorrow what can be done today – tomorrow it
may be illegal.   Anon

FAITH, SIR, WE ARE HERE TODAY, AND GONE TOMORROW.   APHRA BEHN *THE LUCKY CHANCE* (c. 1680)

A bore is someone who is here today, here tomorrow.   Binnie Barnes

On book returns – Gone today, here tomorrow.   Alfred Knopf

Chili today and hot tamale.   Anon

TODAY'S EGG IS TOMORROW'S HEN.   TURKISH PROVERB

Today's shocks are tomorrow's conventions.   Carolyn Wells

Today's gossip is tomorrow's headlines.   Walter Winchell

Don't pay attention to bad reviews. Today's newspaper is tomorrow's
toilet paper: Jack Warner

Today's witty conversationalist is tomorrow's bore.   Anne Scott-James

Yesterday's dancing metaphors are today's clichés. Yesterday's
obscenities are today's banalities.   Arthur Koestler *The Hell of Achilles* (1974)

Yesterday's newspapers are today's fish and chip wrappers.   Anon

Yesterday's luxuries are today's debts.   Anon

———— **"TOOLS"** ————

GIVE US THE TOOLS AND WE SHALL FINISH THE JOB.   SIR WINSTON CHURCHILL (1941)

We have finished the job, what shall we do with the tools? Haile Selassie

THREE – II

There are only three basic jokes, but since the mother-in-law joke is not a joke but a very serious question, there are only two. George Ade

There are three things a woman ought to look: straight as a dart, supple as a snake, and proud as a tiger lily.
Elinor Glyn *The Sayings of Grandmama and Others* (1908)

There are three kinds of pianists: Jewish pianists, homosexual pianists, and bad pianists. Vladimir Horowitz

Three be the things I shall love till I die:
Laughter and hope and a sock in the eye.
Dorothy Parker *Three Things I Love* (1930)

Don't you know, as the French say, there are three sexes: men, women, and clergymen. Sydney Smith

Three things the English public never forgives: youth, power, and enthusiasm. Oscar Wilde

Three things are not to be trusted: a dog's tooth, a horse's hoof, and a baby's bottom. French proverb (c. 1200)

The three sure signs of getting old are losing one's memory . . . Anon

There are three stages in American history: the passing of the buffalo, the passing of the Indian, and the passing of the buck. Anon

❝ TOP ❞

SURREY WITH A FRINGE ON TOP.
RODGERS AND HAMMERSTEIN *SONG TITLE*

Surrey with a whinge on top. Julie Burchill

A crew cut is a furry with a singe on top. Anon

Surrey has a lunatic fringe on top. Graffiti

THERE IS ALWAYS ROOM AT THE TOP. DANIEL WEBSTER

There is room at the top – after the investigation. Oliver Herford

There is plenty of room at the top, but not enough to sit down.
Fred Shero (1975)

There's room at the top, maybe, but only for the clever ones.
Margaret Drabble *Middle Ground* (1980)

There is room at the top because some people who get there go to sleep and roll off. Anon

There is always a rumour at the top. Colin M. Jarman

❝ TOUGH ❞

WHEN THE GOING GETS TOUGH, THE TOUGH GET GOING. KNUTE ROCKNE

When the going gets weird, the weird get going. Hunter S. Thompson

When the tough get going, the weak get screwed. Michael Monroe (1989)

My school motto was *Monsanto incorpori glorius maximia copia* which in Latin means, *When the going gets tough, the tough go shopping.*
Robin Williams *Playboy* (1982)

❝ TRAGEDY ❞

ALL WOMEN BECOME LIKE THEIR MOTHERS. THAT IS THEIR TRAGEDY. NO MAN DOES. THAT IS HIS.
OSCAR WILDE *THE IMPORTANCE OF BEING EARNEST* (1895)

All women dress like their mothers. That is their tragedy. No man does. That is his. Quentin Crisp

❝ TREE ❞

**I THINK THAT I SHALL NEVER SEE
A POEM AS LOVELY AS A TREE.** JOYCE KILMER *TREES*

I think that I shall never see
   A billboard lovely as a tree. Ogden Nash *Song of the Open Road*

❝ TRIUMPH ❞

A SECOND MARRIAGE IS ANOTHER INSTANCE OF THE TRIUMPH OF HOPE OVER EXPERIENCE
SAMUEL JOHNSON

Sky One TV is a triumph of soap over experience.
Philip Reevell *The Guardian* (1993)

A TRIUMPH OF MIND OVER MATTER. ANON SAYING

Women represent the triumph of matter over mind, just as men represent the triumph of mind over morals.
Oscar Wilde *The Picture of Dorian Gray* (1890)

Love is the triumph of imagination over intelligence. H. L. Mencken

Television is a triumph of equipment over people.   Fred Allen

Age is a triumph of mind over matter. If you don't mind, it doesn't matter.   Dan Ingman

Poetry is the triumph of mind over metre.   Anon

Sales resistance is the triumph of mind over patter.   Anon

Modesty is the triumph of mind over flatter.   Anon

❝ TROUBLE ❞

NOBODY KNOWS THE TROUBLE I'VE SEEN. NOBODY KNOWS BUT JESUS.   NEGRO SPRITUAL SONG (1865)

On opera-singer Helen Traubels – Nobody knows the Traubels I've seen.   Rudolf Bing

A TROUBLE SHARED IS A TROUBLE HALVED.   PROVERB

A trouble shared is a trouble dragged out till bedtime.   Victoria Wood

❝ TRUMPET ❞

BLOW ONE'S OWN TRUMPET.   DIOGENES LAERTIUS *ADAGIA* (125)

The fellow is blowing his own strumpet.   W. S. Gilbert

Get someone else to blow your own trumpet and the sound will carry twice as far.   Will Rogers

❝ TRUST ❞

IN GOD HAVE I PUT MY TRUST.   PSALMS *THE BIBLE*

Put your trust in God, but tie your camel first.   Persian Proverb

In God we trust is only another way of saying that we will chance it.   Samuel Butler *Notebooks* (1912)

In gold have I put my trust.   Anon

In God we trust, but all others pay cash.   Anon

❝ TRUTH ❞

'TIS STRANGE – BUT TRUE; FOR TRUTH IS ALWAYS STRANGE, – STRANGER THAN FICTION.

LORD BYRON *DON JUAN* (1823)

Fact is stranger than fiction.   Augustus Jessop (1881)

Truth is stranger than fiction to some people, but I am measurably familiar with it.   Mark Twain (1893)

The chap who said that truth is stranger than fiction died before fiction reached its present state of development.   *Elmira Star Gazette*

Facts may be stranger than fiction, but fiction is generally truer than facts.   E. J. Millward *Copper Bottle* (1929)

Truth is not only stranger than fiction but far more interesting.

Margaret Echard (1943)

Youth is stranger than fiction.   J. D. Fenna

Fact is richer than diction.   J. L. Austin

Truth is stranger than fiction, but not so popular.   Anon

Truth is stranger than fiction, and a lot cleaner.   Anon

THE TRUTH IS MIGHTY, AND IT PREVAILS.   *VULGATE*

On baseball player 'Babe' Ruth – The Ruth is mighty and shall prevail.

Heywood Broun

❝ TWO ❞

FOR WHERE TWO OR THREE ARE GATHERED TOGETHER IN MY NAME, THERE AM I IN THE MIDST OF THEM.   MATTHEW 18:20 *THE BIBLE*

Where two of three are gathered together – that is about enough.

Les A. Murray *Company*

IT TAKES TWO TO QUARREL.   SOCRATES (406 BC)

It takes two to speak the truth – one to speak, and another to hear.

Henry D. Thoreau

It takes two to quarrel and it takes two to make peace also.

Alexander MacLaren (1912)

In spite of the saying, it takes in reality only one to make a quarrel. It is useless for the sheep to pass resolutions in favour of vegetarianism, while the wolf remains of a different opinion.

Dean W. R. Inge (1919)

It takes two to make a murder. There are born victims, born to have their throats cut.   Aldous Huxley *Point Counter Point* (1928)

It takes two to make a marriage a success and only one a failure.

Herbert Samuel

It takes two to make trouble for one.   Mae West

There are lots of things you can do alone! But, it takes two to tango.

Hoffman and Manning *Takes Two to Tango* (1952)

It takes two teams to make a final – and Widnes have done just that.

Ray French

It takes two to tandem.   Judy Hughes *The Guardian* (1993)

THE NOTION IS AS CLEAR AS THAT TWO AND TWO MAKES FOUR.   JEREMY COLLIER (1697)

The formula two and two makes five is not without its attractions.

Fyodor Dostoyevsky

Even in the valley of death, two and two do not make six.   Leo Tolstoy

Under the new math 2 and 2 sometimes make 22. Obviously, the new math is well suited for interpreting the new economics.

Harry Karns *Newsday*

The difference between a psychopath and a neurotic is that a psychopath thinks two plus two is five, while a neurotic knows two plus two is four, but he worries about it.   Anon

Mediocrity adds two to two and only gets four.   Anon

Discretion is putting two and two together and keeping your mouth shut.   Anon

THERE ARE ONLY TWO FAMILIES IN THE WORLD, THE HAVES AND THE HAVE-NOTS.

MIGUEL DE CERVANTES *DON QUIXOTE* (1615)

We have developed an affluent society in which people are divided not so much between haves and have-nots, as between haves and have-mores.   R. A. Butler (1960)

There are two kind of cruise-ship passenger – the heaves and the
heave-nots.   Coleen Pifer

There are only two kinds of people – the haves and the have-nots – or
to put it more simply – wives and husbands.   Anon

TWO ARE BETTER THAN ONE.   ARISTOTLE (330 BC)

Two are better than one – but the man who said that did not know
my sisters.   Samuel Butler

**TWO HALF-TRUTHS DO NOT MAKE A TRUTH, AND
TWO HALF-CULTURES DO NOT MAKE A CULTURE.**
                    ARTHUR KOESTLER *THE GHOST IN THE MACHINE* (1967)

Two halfwits do not make a wit.   Neil Kinnock

TWO HALVES MAKE A WHOLE.   MATHEMATICAL PRECEPT

Two halves make a hole and the fullback goes through.
                                              American football maxim

**YOU'D LOOK SWEET UPON THE SEAT OF A BICYCLE
MADE FOR TWO.**   HARRY DACRE *DAISY BELL*

You'd look sweet upon the seat of a bisexual made for two.   Anon

—— ❝ UGLY ❞ ——

**BEING ATTACKED ON CHARACTER BY GOVERNOR
CLINTON IS LIKE BEING CALLED UGLY BY A FROG.**
                                        GEORGE BUSH (1992)

Being called a political bungler by Cecil Parkinson is rather like being
called ugly by Ross Perot.   'The Weasel' *Independent on Sunday* (1992)

—— ❝ UNDERSTANDING ❞ ——

**THE PEACE OF GOD, WHICH PASSETH ALL
UNDERSTANDING.**   PHILIPPIANS 4:7 *THE BIBLE*

John Donne's poems are like the peace of God: they pass all understanding.   King James I

Neville Chamberlain's 'Peace in our time' is the peace that passeth all
understanding.   Anon (1941)

Skool food or the piece of cod which passeth understanding.
          Geoffrey Willans and Ronald Searle *The Compleet Molesworth* (1958)

TWO – I

There are two kinds of people in the world – those who divide the world into two kinds of people and those who don't.   Robert Benchley

There are two things that I have always loved madly: women and celibacy.   Nicholas de Chamfort

In England there are only two climates: winter and winter.
                                            Shelagh Delaney *A Taste of Honey* (1959)

There are two sorts of reader: one who carefully goes through a book, and the other who as carefully lets the book go through him.
                                                                    Douglas Jerrold

Women complain about sex more than men. Their gripes fall into two major categories: not enough and too much.   Ann Landers

The world is divided into people who do things and those who get the credit.   Dwight Merrow

There are two things no man will admit he can't do well: drive a car and make love.   Stirling Moss

There are just two people entitled to refer to themselves as *we*; one is an editor and the other is a fellow with a tapeworm.   Edgar W. Nye

People ought to be one of two things: young or old. No! What's the use of fooling? People ought to be one of two things: young or dead.   Dorothy Parker

There are two kinds of women: goddesses and doormats.   Pablo Picasso

The world is inhabited by two species of human being: mankind and the English.   Dr G. Renier

There are two motives for reading a book: one, that you enjoy it; the other, that you can boast about it.   Bertrand Russell

There are only two things a child will share willingly: communicable diseases and his mother's age.   Dr Benjamin Spock

There are two things that don't last long: dogs that chase cars and professional golfers who putt for pars.   Lee Trevino

The world is divided into the people who think they are right.   Anon

Women come in two types: young and not so young.
                                                        Anon advertising maxim

There are two kinds of pedestrian: the quick and the dead.   Anon

TWO – II

There are two occasions when a closed mouth can be of help to you:
when you're about to say something against a person, and when
you're offered dessert.   O. A. Battista *Quotoons*

There are two kinds of fool: those who can't change their mind and
those who won't.   Josh Billings

There are two kinds of job: those where you shower before work, and
those where you shower after.   Gary Daley

There are only two styles of portrait painting; the serious and the
smirk.   Charles Dickens

There are two kinds of women: those who want power in the world,
and those who want power in bed.   Jaqueline Kennedy Onassis

There are two modes of transport in Los Angeles: car and ambulance.
                                           Fran Lebowitz *Social Studies*

A boxer makes a comeback for one of two reasons: either he's broke
or he needs the money.   Alan Minter

There are two kinds of people in the world: those who like Neil
Diamond and those who don't like Neil Diamond.
                                        Bill Murray *What About Bob?* (1990)

There are only two sorts of doctors: those who practice with their
brains, and those who practice with their tongues.   William Osler

I was the toast of two continents: Greenland and Australia.
                                                         Dorothy Parker

There are two kinds of loser: the good loser and the one who can't
act.   Laurence J. Peter *The Peter Principle*

There are only two kinds of men: the dead and the deadly. Helen Rowland

Science is divided into two categories: physics and stamp-collecting.
                                                       Ernest Rutherford

There are two kinds of statistics, the kind you look up and the kind
you make up.   Rex Stout *Death of a Doxy*

There are only two terrors on a plane: boredom and terror. Orson Welles

There are only two kinds of people who are really fascinating: people
who know everything, and people who know nothing.   Oscar Wilde

The only two jobs that are paid to run people down are: critics and
elevator operators.   Anon

Two things never to be believed: how a man got a black eye and how
a girl got a mink coat.   Anon

There are two kinds of women: those who take what you are, and
those who take what you have.   American saying

" VARIETY "

VARIETY'S THE SPICE OF LIFE.

WILLIAM COWPER *THE TASK* (1785)

Variety is the spice of love. Helen Rowland (1913)

Variety is the vice of wives. Phyllis McGinley (1940)

Surprise is the variety of life, you know. R.A.J. Watling (1943)

Interruptions are the spice of life. Don Herold

Compromise, if not the spice of life, is its solidity.
Phyllis McGinley *Suburbia* (1959)

Gossip columnists are the spies of life. Doris Dolphin

Spice is the variety of life. Jimmy Saville

Zanzibar is the life of spice. *Observer* (1994)

Variety's the life of spies. Anon

Variety may be the spice of life, but it is good old monotony that buys
the groceries. Anon

" VICTOR "

TO THE VICTOR BELONG THE SPOILS. PROPERTIUS (22 BC)

The victor belongs to the spoils. F. Scott Fitzgerald

To the victor belong the toils. Adlai Stevenson

One trouble with the world is that there are always more victors than
spoils. Anon

" VIRTUE "

PATIENCE IS THE VIRTUE OF THE POOR.

RICHARD FLECKNOE (1656)

Patriotism is the virtue of the vicious. Oscar Wilde

Punctuality is the virtue of the bored. Evelyn Waugh *Diary* (1976)

VIRTUE IS ITS OWN REWARD. CLAUDIAN (399)

Virtue is its own disappointment. Philip Moeller (1841)

Virtue is its own reward, but not at the box office. Mae West

Virtue is its own revenge. E. Y. Harburg

Virtue is its own reward, but have you ever realized what a damned poor reward it may be? Percival Wilde (1940)

If virtue is its own reward, who blames man for wandering farther afield? *Meditations in Wall Street* (1940)

Vice is its own reward. Quentin Crisp *The Naked Civil Servant* (1968)

❝ VOICE ❞

THE VOICE OF THE PEOPLE IS THE VOICE OF GOD. (*VOX POPULI VOX DEI*) ALCUIN *WORKS* (804)

The people's voice is odd,
It is, and it is not, the voice of God. Alexander Pope *To Augustus* (1737)

The voice of the people is the voice of the humbug. (*Vox populi vox humbug*) General W. T. Sherman (1863)

❝ WAGES ❞

THE WAGES OF SIN IS DEATH. ROMANS 6:23 *THE BIBLE*

The wages of sin is alimony. Carolyn Wells

The wages of sin and the reward for virtue are not so different. Joseph Shearing (1932)

The wages of sin is an income for life. William Irish (1943)

The wages of gin is breath. L. L. Levinson

The wages of sin are increased [newspaper] circulation. Lord Ardwick (1989)

The wages of sin are unreported. Anon

The wages of sin may be death, but the hours are great! Anon

The wages of sin are never frozen. Anon

" WAITS "

EVERYTHING COMES TO HE WHO WAITS.

ALEXANDER BARCLAY *ECLOGUES* (1513)

Everything comes to him who hustles while he waits.   Thomas A. Edison

Ah, 'All things come to those who wait,' . . .
They come, but often come too late.   Violet Fane (1890)

Everything comes to those who know how to wait.

Lord Avebury *Use of Life* (1894)

Everything comes to him who waits, but a loaned book.   Kin Hubbard

Everything comes to him who waits, among other things – death.

Francis H. Bradley

Everything comes to him who waits for taxi-cabs on rainy days –
except taxi-cabs.   *Judge*

All things come to him whose name is on a mailing list.   *Classic Puzzles*

Even a waiter finally comes to him who waits.   Anon

Everything comes to him who waits, except the time he lost waiting.

Anon

Everything comes to him who waits, but not soon enough.   Anon

Everything comes to him who crosses the street against a red light.

Anon

Everything comes to him who waits, but most of us aren't sure what
we are waiting for.   Anon

Everything comes to the other person if you sit down and wait.   Anon

TIME AND TIDE WAIT FOR NO MAN.   ROBERT GREENE (1596)

Time and tide wait for no man, but time always stands still for a
woman of thirty.   Robert Frost

Time and tide and newspapers wait for no man.

C. Aird *Some Die Eloquent* (1979)

Diarrhoea waits for no man.   Graffiti

" WALKS "

I WORSHIPPED THE VERY GROUND SHE WALKED ON.

CHARLES DICKENS *WRECK GOLDEN MARY* (1856)

I'm a fan of Richard Nixon, I worship the quicksand he walks on.

Art Buchwald (1974)

On US naval captain Barney Kelly (after he had allowed the USS Enterprise to run ashore in San Francisco Bay) – He grounds the warship he walks on.   John Bracken (1983)

—————— ❝ WALL ❞ ——————

THE WRITING'S ON THE WALL.   ANON SAYING

On baseball players – The handwriting is on the wall, but these
   athletes can't read.   Charlie Finley

On Jean-Marie Le Pen (French politician) – Would you say the
   writing's on the wall for Le Pen?   Peter Deeley

Graffiti is the rioting on the wall.   Graffiti

—————— ❝ WAR ❞ ——————

'CRY HAVOC!' AND LET SLIP THE DOGS OF WAR.
                         WILLIAM SHAKESPEARE *JULIUS CAESAR* (1599)

On The French Foreign Legion – Let slip the frogs of war.
                                            A. A. Gill *Sunday Times* (1993)

WAR IS MUCH TOO SERIOUS A THING TO BE LEFT
TO THE GENERALS.   CHARLES M. DE TALLEYRAND Attrib. (c. 1815)

Youth is a wonderful thing; what a crime to waste it on children.
                                                              G. B. Shaw

I have come to the conclusion that politics is too serious a matter to
   be left to the politicians.   Charles de Gaulle

History is too serious to be left to historians.   Iain MacLeod

Broadcasting is really too important to be left to broadcasters.
                                                              Tony Benn

Architecture is too important to be left to architects alone. Like crime,
   it is a problem for society as a whole.   Berthold Lubetkin (1985)

—————— ❝ WASH ❞ ——————

ONE DOES NOT WASH ONE'S DIRTY LINEN IN
PUBLIC.   NAPOLEON BONAPARTE Attrib.

The amount of women in London who flirt with their own husbands
   is perfectly scandalous. It looks bad. It is simply washing one's own
   clean linen in public.   Oscar Wilde *The Importance of Being Earnest* (1895)

" WATER "

BLOOD IS THICKER THAN WATER.

EURIPIDES *ANDROMACHE* (426 BC)

Blood is thicker than water – and dirtier.

Richard Shattuck *The Snark was a Boojum* (1941)

Mud is thicker than water. L. L. Levinson

The Middle East is where oil is thicker than water. James Holland

" WEB "

O, WHAT A TANGLED WEB WE WEAVE,
WHEN FIRST WE PRACTISE TO DECEIVE!

SIR WALTER SCOTT *MARMION* (1808)

Oh, what a tangled web we weave
When first we practise to conceive.

Don Herold

Oh, what a tangled web do parents weave
When they think that their children are naive.

Ogden Nash

Here's a truth men can perceive
As wholly everlasting:
Oh, what a tangled web they weave
When first they practise fly casting.

Annis Poland

" WHEAT "

TILL FROM THE STRAW THE FLAIL THE CORN DOTH
BEAT, UNTIL THE CHAFF BE SEPARATED FROM THE
WHEAT. GEORGE WHITER *FRAGMENTA POETICA*

An editor is one who separates the wheat from the chaff and prints
the chaff. Adlai Stevenson

On Geoffrey Wheatcroft's 'Absent Friends' (1989) – Separating the
wheat from the naff. *Private Eye*

" WHITE "

TWO BLACKS DO NOT MAKE A WHITE. SCOTTISH PROVERB
Two black eyes won't make a white one.   G. B. Shaw *Major Barbara* (1905)

" WHO "

WHO IS SYLVIA? WHAT IS SHE?
WILLIAM SHAKESPEARE *THE TWO GENTLEMEN OF VERONA* (1594)
Who is Sylvia? What? Is she?   Anon

" WHOLE "

THE WHOLE IS MORE THAN THE SUM OF THE PARTS.   ARISTOTLE (c. 350 BC)
Democracy is an institution in which the whole is equal to the scum of
the parts.   Keith Preston

" WIFE "

BIGAMY IS HAVING ONE WIFE TOO MANY.
MONOGAMY IS THE SAME.   OSCAR WILDE (c. 1900)
Bigamy is having one life too many.   Anon
Monotony is having one wife too many.   Anon
THAT'S NO LADY, THAT'S MY WIFE.   ANON SAYING
That's no laity, that's my wife.   Dorothy Parker

" WILL "

JOHN STUART MILL,
BY A MIGHTY EFFORT OF WILL,
OVERCAME HIS NATURAL BONHOMIE,
AND WROTE *PRINCIPLES OF POLITICAL ECONOMY*.
E. C. BENTLEY *BIOGRAPHY FOR BEGINNERS*

John Stuart Mill,
Of his own free will,
On a half-a-pint of shandy
Was particularly ill.   Monty Python's Flying Circus *The Bruce Song*

WHERE THERE'S A WILL, THERE'S A WAY.

GEORGE HERBERT *OUTLANDISH PROVERBS* (1640)

Man has his will, but woman has her way.

Oliver W. Holmes *The Autocrat of the Breakfast Table*

When there is no will, there is no way for lawyers.   Austin O'Malley

Where there's a will, there's a lot of greedy relatives.

Bill Cosby *You Bet Your Life* (1993)

Where there's a will, there's trouble.   Anon

Where there's a will, there's a wail.   Anon

❝ WIND ❞

IT'S AN ILL WIND THAT BLOWS NO GOOD.

JOHN HEYWOOD *PROVERBS* (1546)

It is an ill wind that blows when you leave the hairdresser.   Phyllis Diller

An oboe is an ill woodwind that blows no good.   Anon

❝ WINE ❞

NEITHER DO MEN PUT NEW WINE INTO OLD BOTTLES; ELSE THE BOTTLES BREAK.

MATTHEW *THE BIBLE*

I think the British have the distinction above all other nations of being
able to put new wine into old bottles without bursting them.

Clement Attlee *Time* (1950)

WINE, WOMEN AND SONG.   PLUTARCH (95)

A bachelor is a guy who believes in wine, women and so long.

John Travolta

I lead a life of wine, women and song – it's cheaper than gas, food
and rent.   Larry Fields *Philadelphia News*

Ashore it's wine, women and song;
Aboard, it's rum, bum and the concertina.   Naval saying

—— 66 WINNING 99 ——

WINNING ISN'T EVERYTHING, IT IS THE ONLY THING.

(This is a hybrid of two quotes from American sports coaches . . .
WINNING ISN'T EVERYTHING, but making the effort is.

VINCE LOMBARDI

I do not think that winning is the most important thing, *I think IT IS
    THE ONLY THING.*   BILL VEECK)

Winning is not only not everything, winning is not anything.

George Leonard

Winning in politics isn't everything, it's the only thing.

Richard Nixon presidential campaign slogan (1972)

Winning may not be everything, but it sure as hell beats the dog shit
    out of what comes second.   American football saying

—— 66 WINTER 99 ——

NOW IS THE WINTER OF OUR DISCONTENT
MADE GLORIOUS SUMMER BY THIS SUN OF YORK.

WILLIAM SHAKESPEARE *RICHARD III* (1595)

Now is the winter of our discontent made glorious summer by central
    heating.   Jack Sharkey

Now is the winter of our discount tent.   January Sales Camping Store slogan

—— 66 WOMAN 99 ——

WHEN LOVELY WOMAN STOOPS TO FOLLY
AND FINDS TOO LATE THAT MEN BETRAY,
WHAT CHARM CAN SOOTHE HER MELANCHOLY,
WHAT ART WASH HER GUILT AWAY?

OLIVER GOLDSMITH *THE VICAR OF WAKEFIELD* (1766)

When lovely woman stoops to folly and
Paces about her room again, alone
She smoothes her hair with automatic hand,
And puts on a gramophone.   T. S. Eliot *The Fire Sermon* (1922)

When lovely woman stoops to folly
The evening can be awfully jolly.   Mary Demetriadis

A WOMAN'S PLACE IS IN THE HOME.   J. SLICK (1844)

A woman's place is in the hay.   Clifford Odets *Golden Boy* (1937)

A woman's place is in the wrong.   James Thurber

A woman's place is in the home warming her husband's slippers.
                                        Colonel Frank Weldon

The suffragettes were triumphant. A woman's place is in the gaol.
                                                Caryl Brahms

A woman's place is in the home – or anyway in some cosy nightclub.
                                                Lucille Ball

A woman's place is in the House – and the Senate.
                                        American feminist slogan

A WOMAN WITHOUT A MAN IS LIKE A FISH
WITHOUT A BICYCLE.   GLORIA STEINEM Attrib. (c. 1970)

A woman without a man is like a fish without a bicycle. Yes, but who
    needs a stationary haddock?   Anon

A woman without a man is like a moose without a hatrack.   Anon

A man without a woman is like a neck without a pain.   Anon

Behind every successful man is a fish with a bicycle.   Graffiti

Man needs God like a goldfish needs a motorbike.   Graffiti

—— **" WON OR LOST "** ——

FOR WHEN THE ONE GREAT SCORER COMES
TO MARK AGAINST YOUR NAME,
HE WRITES – NOT THAT YOU WON OR LOST –
BUT HOW YOU PLAYED THE GAME.
                        GRANTLAND RICE *ALUMNUS FOOTBALL*

For when the one great scorer comes
To mark against your name,
It matters not who won or lost
But how you placed the blame.   Blaine Nye (1976)

For when the one great scorer comes
To mark against your name
It matters not who won or lost
But whether you beat England.   Max Boyce

" WOODPILE "

NO NIGGER IN THE WOODPILE HERE . . . WHITE MEN ARE AT THE BOTTOM OF THIS SPECULATION.
KANSAS HISTORY QUARTERLY (1852)

There's an enigma in the woodpile.   Christopher Morley *Kitty Foyle* (1939)

He's the nigger in the stockpile.   Leslie Ford (1944)

Unfortunately, there have been a few niggles in the woodpile, in the last few years.   Ray Illingworth

" WORD "

IN THE BEGINNING WAS THE WORD, AND THE WORD WAS WITH GOD, AND THE WORD WAS GOD.
JOHN 1:1 *THE BIBLE*

In the beginning was nonsense, and the nonsense was with God, and the nonsense was God.   Friedrich Nietzsche

The word is the verb, and the verb is God.   Victor Hugo

In the beginning was the word, and by the mutations came the gene.
Michael A. Arbib

In the beginning was the word, and at the end just the cliché.
Stanislaw J. Lec

In the beginning was not the Levy. In the beginning was horse racing and it managed for three centuries without a levy.
Sir Ian Trethowen (1987)

In the beginning was the word, and the word was aardvark.   Graffiti

KIND WORDS CAN NEVER DIE.   J. FOLEY

Kind words will never die – neither will they buy groceries. Edgar W. Nye

Kind words will never die but without kind deeds they can sound mighty sick.   Anon

MANY A TRUE WORD IS SPOKEN IN JEST.
SCOTTISH PROVERB (c. 1300)

Many a true word is spoken through false teeth.   Anon

‹‹ WORK ››

ALL WORK AND NO PLAY MAKES JACK A DULL BOY.

PROVERB

All work and no play makes Jack a dull boy;
All play and no work makes Jack a mere toy.

Maria Edgeworth *Harry and Lucy Concluded* (1825)

All work and no play makes Jack a dull boy, but all play and no
work makes him something greatly worse. Samuel Smiles *Self-Help* (1859)

He made plenty of jack while they were being dull boys.

Stanley Walker (1941)

All work and no play makes Jack's wife a wealthy widow. T. McDermott

All work and no play means you make money hand over fist.

John Peers *1001 Logical Laws* (1979)

All talk and no pussy makes Jack a dull boy. American saying

All work and no spree makes Jill a dull she. American saying

A returned dramatic manuscript is a case of all work and no play. Anon

All work and no play makes jack for the nerve specialist. Anon

HARD WORK NEVER HURT ANYBODY. PROVERB

They say hard work never hurt anybody, but I figure why take the
chance. Terence Rattigan

Hard work never hurt anybody, but it may frighten some people to
death. Anon

Hard work never hurt anybody who doesn't have to do it. Anon

A WOMAN'S WORK IS NEVER DONE.

THOMAS TUSSER *HUSBANDRY* (1570)

A woman's work is to delegate. John Cleese

A woman's word is never done. Anon

A woman's work is never done when it never gets started! Anon

A woman's work is never done
As gossiping is far more fun. Anon

A woman's work is never done by a man. Graffiti (1980)

" WORLD "

STOP THE WORLD, I WANT TO GET OFF.

ANTHONY NEWLEY AND LESLIE BRICUSSE *MUSICAL TITLE* (1961)

Stop Miss World – we want to get off. Feminist protest slogan

THIS IS THE WAY THE WORLD ENDS NOT WITH A BANG BUT A WHIMPER.
T.S. ELIOT *THE HOLLOW MEN* (1925)

The world is going to end, not with a wimp but a banker. Paul Desmond

WORKERS OF THE WORLD, UNITE!

KARL MARX *THE COMMUNIST MANIFESTO* (1848)

Arsonists of the world, ignite. Anon

Grandmothers of the world, you knit. Colin M. Jarman

" WRONG "

ANYTHING THAT CAN GO WRONG, WILL GO WRONG.
MURPHY'S LAW

If anything can't go wrong, it might. Anon

On her popularity in Europe as a burlesque entertainer –
FIFTY MILLION FRENCHMEN CAN'T BE WRONG.

TEXAS GUINAN Attrib (c. 1931)

Fifty million Frenchmen can't be right. G. B. Shaw

One hundred million lemmings can't be wrong. Anon

TWO WRONGS WILL NOT MAKE A RIGHT.

GABRIEL HARVEY (1593)

Three wrongs will not make one right. Benjamin Rush *Letter* (1783)

Richard Nixon's motto was: If two wrongs don't make a right, try
three. Norman Cousins

Two wrongs never make a riot. L. L. Levinson

Two wrongs don't make a right, but they make a good excuse.
Thomas Szasz

On Australian immigration law – Two Wongs don't make a white.
Arthur Calwell

If two wrongs do not make a right, three rights can make a terrible
wrong. *Daily Telegraph* (1979)

Bigamy is a case of two rites making a wrong. Anon

INDEX

Gissing, George 127
Gleason, Jackie 136
Glyn, Elinor 113, 183
Godard, Jean-Luc 61, 63
Goethe, Johann Wolfgang von 106
Goetz, A. O. 96
Gogarty, Oliver St. John 71
Gold, Herb 62
Goldman, R. L. 97
Goldman, William 59
Goldsmith, Oliver 30, 198
Goldwyn, Samuel 27, 33, 89
Good, Dr. I. J. 47
Goodman, John 97
Goodwin, J. Cheever 26
Gordon, Jane 35
Gordon, Mitchell 46
Gordon, Richard 15, 114, 177
Gould, Bryan 102
Goward, Pru 117
Gracian, Baltasaar 16, 55
Graffiti 12, 14, 19, 24, 25, 26, 30,
    32, 35, 37, 43, 47, 52, 58, 59, 60,
    61, 66, 67, 77, 78, 79, 81, 82, 85,
    86, 91, 92, 94, 95, 96, 97, 112,
    114, 115, 116, 118, 119, 120, 122,
    123, 124, 128, 130, 132, 135, 138,
    140, 142, 155, 156, 167, 170, 172,
    173, 174, 176, 178, 179, 183, 193,
    194, 199, 200, 201
Graman, Jean 173
Grand, James 99
Grant, Russell 172
Gray, Thomas 100, 145
Gregory, Horace 123
Greene, Robert 193
Greenaway, P. van 178
Greenspun, Roger 103
Gregory, Dick 93
Griffiths, Leon 142
Griffiths, Trevor 109

Grison, Campbell 103
Guardian 47, 60, 69, 87
Gubba, Tony 107
Guedella, Philip 19, 52, 95, 124,
    125, 165
Guinan, Texas 202
Gumperson's Law 148
Guthrie, Jim 16
Guyon, Albe 94

H

Haile Selassie 182
Hague, Frank 157
Hailsham, Lord 158
Haisey, Wayne 22
Hale, Christopher 30
Hale, Sarah J. 138
Haliburton, T. C. 113
Hall, Arsenio 51, 128
Hamilton, Alexander 116
Hammerstein II, Oscar 168
Hancock, Sheila 71
Handeau, Marcel 106
Harburg, E. Y. 88, 192
Harding, Gilbert 124
Hardy, Oliver 124
Hare, David 13
Harkness, Richard 44
Harmsworth, Geoffrey 52
Harper's Magazine 39
Harpur, Marrily 149
Harriman, Averell 89
Harris, Arnold 162
Harris, Richard 54
Harris, Sydney 63
Harrison, Sarah 91
Hartson, William 92
Harvey, Gabriel 202
Haskins, Henry H. 54, 97
Hatton, Derek 88, 129
Haugaard, Kay 162